RICE UNIVERSITY STUDIES

ISSUES IN INCOME DISTRIBUTION

RONALD SOLIGO AND FRED R. VON DER MEHDEN, Editors

STEPHEN O. BENDER
ROBERT H. DIX
MALCOLM GILLIS
YHI-MIN HO
DONALD L. HUDDLE
MARIAN KRZYZANIAK
UZIR MALIK
CHARLES E. McLURE, JR.
GASTON RIMLINGER
GORDON W. SMITH
RONALD SOLIGO
WAYNE R. THIRSK
FRED R. VON DER MEHDEN

PUBLISHED BY
WILLIAM MARSH RICE UNIVERSITY
HOUSTON, TEXAS

Vol. 61, No. 4 Fall 1975

US-ISSN-0035-4996
US-ISBN-0-89263-226-7

RICE UNIVERSITY STUDIES

Vol. 61, No. 4 Fall 1975

ISSUES IN INCOME DISTRIBUTION

INTRODUCTION

The span of years that have elapsed since most of the less developed countries achieved independence and seriously focused on development is extremely short, considering the historical experience of the developed countries. Yet governments of the developing world now believe that they have much less time to achieve modernization and significant increases in living standards than was available to other countries in the past. While it took many decades for the more developed countries to industrialize, most LDCs today are demanding that they show significant change in the structure of their economies and the levels of per capita income in one or two decades.

The impatience with delayed progress is the result, in part, of the rise of politically active and restless groups within the developing economies. These groups have emerged in part because of the relatively recent phenomenon of massive migration of poor and unskilled people from rural areas to the large cities. Large population shifts have created serious problems of unemployment and inadequacy of public services such as water and sanitary facilities. In addition, the contact of poor people with the wealth and life styles of the urban upper and middle classes has raised their awareness of consumption possibilities, has heightened their expectations and demands, and ultimately has crystallized their dissatisfactions and frustrations. Concentrations of dissatisfied people in urban centers pose a serious threat to the stability of governments. The political need to satisfy some of the demands from the urban poor represents a new constraint on the range of policy options available to countries that are now in the earlier stages of development.

At the same time rural areas have become more politicized as communications have expanded the horizon of the previously parochial and politically apathetic rural population. In addition, nationalist movements and post-colonial politics have brought new elements into the political arena and new demands upon the LDC governments.

Additional pressures are coming from a significant local intellectual community, many of whom were trained in the developed countries as a part of the aid policies of the 1950s and 1960s. Such people have been able to articulate the demands of the local poor as well as the demands of their poor nations vis-à-vis the rich countries. They have taken the lead in criticizing and rejecting past policies and in formulating demands for a "new world order."

Finally, LDCs are being forced to take a hard look at their development strategies and to come up with alternatives as a result of the recent and continuing decreases in foreign aid from developed nations, the growing foreign debts of the LDCs, the end of U. S. food surpluses and the phenomenal rise in energy and chemical prices resulting from recent increases in petroleum prices.

The failure of past economic development policies to alter significantly the conditions of abject poverty experienced by the bottom forty to fifty percent of the less developed countries' population and to reverse the growing gap in per capita income between rich and poor countries has, in the last few years, led to a reassessment of those policies and of the developmental models that justified them. The sudden shift in emphasis toward distributional issues has caught social scientists unprepared. Economists, for example, still do not have a widely-held and well-developed theory of income distribution which would explain how distribution is determined at any given time and how it changes over a period of time. Indeed, until very recently there were practically no data on the distribution of income for most LDCs and for earlier periods of the now-industrialized countries, so that it was impossible even to make quantitative comparisons among countries or within a country over a period of time.

Thus it has only been in the last decade that discussions of income distribution have been taken seriously in social science literature. For economists, who traditionally defined economic development as a sustained increase in per capita income, without reference to the distribution of the increase in income, the shift in focus is of even more recent vintage.

The previous lack of interest in income distribution had many origins. First, there was a general consensus that the key problem in less developed countries was to increase the rate of growth of their gross national product. It was assumed that if output grew at a sufficiently rapid rate, employment and the income of the poor would also grow; these goals were considered to be equivalent. Any "bad" connotations of inequality were offset by the argument that it was sufficient to increase everyone's income in absolute terms even if the distribution became more unequal.

Second, there was some belief, supported by the work of Simon Kuznets, that the distribution of income was determined largely by the productive structure of the economy and that the changes in that structure which accompany economic development will, in the early stages of growth, produce more income inequality. The inevitability of a deterioration in distributional equity was made more palatable to egalitarians by the belief that, since the rich save a higher proportion of their income than the poor, higher degrees of inequality would generate a higher savings rate and, hence, a higher rate of output growth, ultimately helping the whole society.

A third factor was the dichotomy between growth on the one hand and equity on the other which has developed in the economic literature in this century. It was believed—a belief which is still strongly held in some developed economies—that the two issues were separable; that economic policy should be organized to maximize the size and growth rate of the economy; any undesirable distributional outcomes could be rectified *ex post facto* by means of tax-transfer schemes of one sort or another. Recognition is only now being given to the overwhelming evidence of the failure of governments to redistribute significant portions of income through fiscal and welfare policies, and to the fact that these policies usually have enormous efficiency costs of their own (e.g., through decreases in incentives to work or take risks).

Consistent with this intellectual orientation, development policies promoted by donor countries and institutions and pursued by developing countries during the post-World War II period neglected distributional issues. Attention was focused on issues such as ways in which domestic savings could be mobilized, foreign exchange earnings enhanced, and foreign exchange use decreased. Policies that grew out of these concerns, such as import substitution, export promotion, or management of foreign exchange rates, were considered almost entirely for their effects on the growth rate of output. Other indicators of success included the ratio of domestic savings to GNP, the ratio of savings to total investments, changes in the level and rates of growth of exports, the ratio of output of manufactured goods to GNP, and so on. If one reads the literature written during the 1950s and 1960s, whether by academics or by practitioners, one is struck by the absence of reference, except in a perfunctory way, to the issue of distributional equity as a criterion for evaluating developmental policies. Furthermore, the literature neglected variables that would measure the benefits accruing to the poor affecting at least their absolute standard of life as opposed to their share of the total. Rather, attention was focused on broad aggregates.

The result of these policy criteria and the policies they inspired was an ever-widening disparity in the incomes of rich and poor nations as a whole and between rich and poor groups within the LDCs. Twenty-five years of unprecedented development efforts often left the majority of the people in the LDCs unaffected or, worse still, left them poorer (as, for example, when the spread of modern industry gradually eliminated the jobs and livelihoods of those engaged in more traditional modes of production). These effects occurred despite significant, albeit limited, success in achieving what are, by historical standards, respectable rates of growth of GNP in the less developed countries.

I

The papers presented in this volume are an outgrowth of four years of research on income distribution carried out by Associates of the Program of Development Studies (PDS) of Rice University. The Program itself is a product of discussions among members of the Departments of Economics and Political Science, begun in 1970, which sought to delineate areas of common concern that might lead to a unified research project. After considerable discussion, the varied interests of the Associates were narrowed to an analysis of the economic, political, and social ramifications of the distribution of gains, wealth, and income in the developing world.

The overall project was begun with an initial grant of seed money from the Menil Foundation and then augmented by sizable research support from the Agency for International Development (AID) and the National Science Foundation. Over the past three years the Program of Development Studies has expanded its membership and research under the general rubric of income distribution. The interdisciplinary nature of its work was reinforced by the inclusion of Rice faculty and graduate students in anthropology, sociology, and architecture, as well as of associates from other universities. Field work was carried out primarily in Colombia, Malaysia, Brazil, and Turkey. Scholars and government officials from the United States and other countries who are interested in income distribution have presented papers and held seminars at Rice. All of this interaction has been subject to critical evaluation of the Associates at regular meetings where research proposals, ongoing research, and results are discussed. The products of these activities have appeared in sixty-six PDS Discussion Papers and twenty-three published articles and monographs (a list of the Discussion Papers follows this introduction).

The Program of Development Studies is now launching a second phase of its income distribution research under a three-year renewal of its AID contract. It is appropriate at this time to present to a general audience the results of our several years of work. It should be emphasized that this small volume can in no way encompass all of the research and analysis accomplished by the Associates of the PDS. Topics of the sixty-six Discussion Papers have ranged from economic analysis of agricultural and tax policies, by economists, through research on communal groups, by anthropologists and political scientists. Our activities in Malaysia and Colombia illustrate the scope of the Program's activities in any one country. In Malaysia, political scientists have analyzed problems of industry, health, and education; anthropologists have studied aspects of expenditures by communal groups; and economists have assessed taxation and market structure. In Colombia the work has included studies by economists of agricultural policies, wages, migration, small-scale industry, and taxation, while students of architecture and political science have investigated housing and political attitudes. Where possible, efforts were made to utilize the interdisciplinary interests of the participants in the Program.

This volume has several objectives. We wanted the papers to reflect the scope of PDS-supported research. Therefore, the individual studies are ordered under three broad headings: 1) the political, social, and economic factors that help to provide the background to problems and programs related to income distribution in particular areas; 2) specific domestic research issues assessed by Associates; and 3) problems that affect the distribution of income and wealth among states within the international community. Secondly, the papers reflect the interests of the Associates as well as the wide geographic range of research. Finally, we have urged the authors to present their work in a manner readable by those outside the respective disciplines. While the particular jargon of economics and political science has been restrained, disciplinary demands have made necessary the inclusion of some nomenclature which may not be entirely familiar to those outside each "fraternity."

II

Outlining the contents of the papers that follow will allow the reader to recognize the relevance of the particular contributions to our general investigation of the distribution of gains, wealth, and income. As noted previously, the first section of this volume is part of an effort to provide general background for the study of particular issues in income distribution. It has been a basic assumption of the Program that it is necessary to understand the fundamental social, economic, and political characteristics of the societies within which we are analyzing more specific income distribution problems. Four papers display different perspectives of this effort.

Professor Rimlinger's paper analyzes the changes in the distribution of income and wealth in tropical Africa that followed the end of colonial rule. It shows which groups have benefited and which have lost from decolonization and assesses the reasons for disparities. Rimlinger notes that while inequalities between Africans and non-Africans have been reduced, inequality among Africans has increased. Factors responsible for the latter phenomenon relate to a complex combination of elements including geographic location, resource bases, government policies, and problems related to post-independence political and economic development. Rimlinger points out patterns of disparity which have appeared in other newly independent states in Afro-Asia, and his concern with growing inequality among Africans is shared by Associates working in Asian states.

Professor Dix's paper is a case study of populism as one kind of political movement that promotes "distributive" justice in reaction to "developmentalist" policies stressing economic growth. The populist movement in question is ANAPO, led by the former Colombian dictator, Gustavo Rojas Pinilla. The paper marshals empirical data on voting patterns to show that although ANAPO has been the most class-based political movement in Colombian history, it is also a "heterogeneous coalition including support from some of the more" conservative groups in Colombia. An examination of ANAPO's leadership, program, and organization bears out its characterization as a modern mass movement retaining persistent elements of traditionalism. In particular its leadership is drawn from the elite groups (albeit the marginal elite groups) and its organization involves the mobilization of groups "from above."

Dix discusses the changes in ANAPO since it nearly won the presidential election in 1970, and speculates on the reasons for the waning of its electoral support. Basically, support for the party has declined as its rhetoric and program have moved to the left.

The importance of Dix's paper in this volume lies in the fact that Colombia (and to some extent other Latin American countries) shows that concern for social justice and distributional equity can be displayed through support for a populist (as distinct from a strictly class- or Marxist-oriented) revolutionary movement. Dix argues that "populism, in the guise of marginal elites mobilizing a heterogeneous mass and unified around a leader, is the typical Latin American reaction to developmentalism." He predicts that such populist movements will continue to characterize political development in Latin America.

Professor von der Mehden's paper is one part of an interdisciplinary effort to provide the political and social background to Malaysia's drive toward narrowing income disparities. While other research has assessed the social and economic roles of particular communal groups in contemporary Malaysia, his study attempts to define the political dynamics that have led to government distributional policies, and especially to understand the actions of interest groups regarding economic programs. He argues that in western democratic states interest groups try primarily to influence the "input" functions of government (i.e., they are engaged in affecting the formulation of legislation and thus attempt to "pressure" voters, legislators, the executive, and, at times, the judiciary). In Malaysia (as in many other less developed states), however, interest groups are primarily engaged in efforts to influence the "output" functions of the country's political system —i.e., to affect the impact upon their firm or organization of laws and regulations already promulgated.

After providing empirical evidence, based upon interviews with Malaysian executives, to support this pattern in Malaysia, von der Mehden discusses the reasons for concentration on output functions. The most important factors include: 1) attitudes antithetical to the activities of western-style interest groups; 2) the tenuous role of the private economic sector; 3) the ownership of firms largely by foreigners and local Chinese; and 4) the existence of other informal means of access to decision-makers.

Professor Soligo focuses on the interrelationship between equity and growth. Because of the increasing pressures for greater distributional equity in less developed economies, it is important to know both the direction and magnitude of the effects of greater equity on other variables such as the growth rate of output and employment. Soligo discusses several approaches. The classical model posits a trade-off between growth and equity. Policies which tilt the distribution of today's income in favor of the low income groups will result in a lower growth rate and a smaller aggregate income in future periods.

A more optimistic approach notes the inefficiencies with which resources are utilized in the typical developing economy, as a result of both undeveloped and imperfect markets and of "bad" economic policies. In this view the adoption of policy changes which improve the efficiency of resource use permits greater output in the aggregate as well as greater output and employment for the lower income groups.

A third approach emphasizes the effects of certain structural characteristics of producer and consumer behavior on the growth-equity relationship. The model discussed in Soligo's paper hypothesizes that lower income families spend a substantial portion of their income on goods and services produced with labor-intensive techniques while the higher income groups tend to spend their income on goods and services requiring relatively more capital. Since LDCs are characterized by an overabundance of unskilled labor but a dearth of capital (both human and tangible capital goods), a shift in the composition of demand towards the more labor-intensive goods would permit the economy, with a given resource endowment, to produce more output, provide more employment, and sustain a more equitable distribution of income. In this model greater equity is consistent with a higher rate of growth in output and employment.

While this last approach is the most optimistic with respect to the possibility of finding alternative development strategies which will lead to an early improvement in the living standards of the poor without sacrificing income levels in the future, its relevance is dependent upon certain assumptions which must be supported or rejected on empirical grounds. Empirical studies which test these assumptions are summarized and the implications of the findings discussed.

The second part of the volume consists of discrete studies of various aspects of income distribution within national polities, presenting examples of the complex nature of the problem in the developing nations. Each of the papers, like those in Part I, is based in part upon field work by the authors, but also reflects an interest in the more technical methodological economic and political issues attendant to the study of income distribution.

Professor Thirsk questions some of the basic solutions usually offered in the developing world to the problem of rural poverty, by analyzing the issue of a trade-off between equity and growth in the context of agricultural policy in Colombia. He argues that while theoretically there is a trade-off, one does not exist in practice because, as a result of policy, the economy is operating well within its efficiency frontier. By changing policy it would be possible to increase efficiency, and hence output, and at the same time increase the incomes of the poor.

Thirsk looks at agricultural price supports, credit allocation policies, farm mechanization, land reform, and rural education. He argues that the elimination of price supports, reallocation of credit towards the smaller farms, and elimination of a subsidy to farm mechanization would lead to an increase in output and a more equal distribution of income. Land redistribution will also lead to an increase in output and will have egalitarian distributive effects (through higher rural employment) in addition to the effects of the redistribution of wealth.

Mr. Bender looks at various alternative solutions to the housing problems of the urban poor in the specific context of Bogotá, Colombia. He considers several types of squatter settlements as well as housing units provided by public agencies. The paper contrasts the traditional view of squatter settlements as blighted areas that must be removed and replaced by institutional means with a more recent view which sees them as viable, adaptive physical environments that allow their occupants to participate in and benefit from development. He also compares these settlements with government sponsored settlements, and finds that the type of growth and change that ultimately results in a mature urban community with a full range of public and private services occurs in both types despite the initial physical constraints imposed by planners in designing the latter.

Finally, Bender emphasizes the fact that home ownership is an important income-generating asset, both from the implicit incomes generated by the housing services provided to the owner-occupier and from the money income received by renting a portion of it to others. In some cases space may be used for commercial enterprises operated by otherwise unemployed members of the family.

The importance of settlement development in permitting the poor to accumulate wealth is influenced by the availability of land, construction materials, and key public services. Changes in any of these factors would affect the rate of settlement development and the ability of the poor to change their living standards under their own initiative. In the case of Bogotá, Bender argues that these elements are changing so as to increase the impediments facing the poor; thus the beneficial outcomes of the past are less likely to be continued into the future.

The contribution of Professors Ho and Huddle results from ongoing research on small-scale and traditional industries, institutions that the authors believe should be encouraged. These firms have important and unique features, including high employment content, location flexibility, and export potential, that could ameliorate some social and economic ills of developing states.

The authors divide small-scale firms into two categories: firms producing non-traditional manufactured goods, which can be produced more efficiently by large-scale methods, and firms producing "handmade goods, artistic products, and other products with distinctive cultural character." The second category holds significant promise as the basis for an alternative development strategy in which employment and income will accrue predominantly to those at the lower end of the economic scale.

Optimism for the future of small-scale firms producing handicrafts and cultural goods is based in part on the growing importance of these goods in international trade. Ho and Huddle find that the demand for these goods by consumers in the developed countries is very elastic, reflecting a desire to acquire nonstandardized, individualized goods and services once more basic needs have been met. On the other hand, small-scale firms are faced with many impediments to their growth. The paper discusses several of these including marketing, financing, and the development of management as well as manufacturing skills.

Professor Krzyzaniak and Mr. Malik are concerned with the effects of market structure and the allocation of property rights on the distribution of income. They discuss, as a case study, the fishing industry in northern W. Malaysia. Noting the importance of fishing for the area and for Malaysia as a whole, they then concentrate their analysis upon distributional problems within the industry itself. The authors state that efforts to control commercial fishing for conservation purposes have led to monopoly through a licensing procedure that has left ownership of the boats and fishing rights in the hands of financiers. When combined with the collusive monopolistic character of the wholesale fish market, the situation produces a very unequal distribution of income in the industry, with the hired fisherman at the bottom. At the same time, fish prices are artificially high, resulting in a further transfer of income from consumers to wholesalers and financiers. Krzyzaniak and Malik call for bringing competition to fish marketing, breaking ties between the retail and wholesale trade, and dispersing ownership of the boats as means of increasing the incomes of the fishermen in particular and consumers as a whole.

The third part of the volume relates to the growing problem of disparities among countries. Both papers in this section note the well-recognized impact of increased petroleum prices on the world economic system. Oil, however, is only one of a variety of natural resources that may affect the international economy, and the OPEC pattern is only one means of dealing with such situations. The paper by Professors Gillis and McLure treats the very complex issue of the distributional implications of taxing natural resources. The authors consider three basic points: 1) the determinants of the incidence of taxation on primary products, 2) conditions under which various types of taxes on primary products can be shifted to nonresidents of the taxing countries, and 3) a case study of Jamaica's tax on bauxite initiated in 1974.

Professor Smith analyzes the employment of internationally held buffer stocks as a means of controlling fluctuations of primary resource commodities, examining copper as his example of the problem. In an effort to evaluate the feasibility of developing a copper buffer stock, Smith used computer simulations of an econometric model of the world copper market. While it is obvious that such econometric simulations give imperfect guidance for the future, they can give order-of-magnitude conclusions which might be employed in using the buffer stock pattern.

RONALD SOLIGO
FRED VON DER MEHDEN
EDITORS

PROGRAM OF DEVELOPMENT STUDIES

Discussion Papers

Discussion Papers are available upon request to individual scholars and researchers and to libraries of educational institutions.

1. "Brazilian Agricultural Policy: 1950-1967" (1969), 70 pp., Gordon Smith.
2. "On the Measurement of Import Substitution" (1969), 19 pp., Samuel A. Morley and Gordon Smith.
3. "International Monetary Rules and External Disequilibrium in Developing Countries" (1969), 19 pp., Donald L. Huddle.
4. "Real and Illusory Aspects of an Overvalued Exchange Rate: The Pakistan Case" (1970), 30 pp., Ronald Soligo.
5. "Import Substitution and Foreign Investment in Brazil" (1970), 25 pp., Samuel A. Morley and Gordon Smith.
6. "Measurements of Static Welfare Losses, Horizontal and Vertical Distribution Inequities, and Revenues in a Multiple Exchange Rate System" (1970), 21 pp., Donald L. Huddle.
7. "National Policy Criteria in a World with International Migration" (1970), 25 pp., R. Albert Berry and Ronald Soligo.
8. "The Role of Government in the Economic Development of Turkey, 1933-63" (1970), 52 pp., James W. Land.
9. "Income Distribution, Employment, and Growth in Labor Redundant Economies" (1971), 37 pp., James W. Land and Ronald Soligo.
10. "The Long-run Incidence of Government Spending on Education" (1970), 24 pp., Marian Krzyzaniak.
11. "Interpreting Domestic Terms of Trade Changes in Pakistan" (1971), 40 pp., Ronald Soligo.
12. "The Design of Regional Tax Incentives for Colombia" (1971), 19 pp., Charles E. McLure, Jr.
13. "Transformation of Polish Agriculture from 1920 On: A Historical Perspective" (1971), 51 pp., Marian Krzyzaniak.
14. "The Incidence of Taxation in Colombia" (1971), 39 pp., Charles E. McLure, Jr.
15. "The Effect of Changes in the Distribution of Income on Labor, Foreign Investment and Growth in Brazil" (1971), 28 pp., S. A. Morley and Gordon Smith.
16. "Korean Rice, Taiwan Rice, and Japanese Agricultural Stagnation: An Economic Consequence of Colonialism—A Comment" (1971), 20 pp., Y. M. Ho.
17. "The Incidence of Taxation in West Malaysia" (1971), 33 pp., Charles E. McLure, Jr.
18. "Vocational Improvement Centres: A Successful Nigerian Experiment" (1971), 24 pp., Gaston V. Rimlinger and Carolyn Stremlau.
19. "Government Expenditures, the Revenue Constraint and Wagner's Law: The Case of Turkey" (1972), 31 pp., Marian Krzyzaniak.

20. Rev. of No. 10. "The Long-run Incidence of Government Spending on Education" (1972), 24 pp., Marian Krzyzaniak and Ibrahim Eris.
21. "On Solow's Method of Estimating the Residual" (1972), 9 pp., Y. M. Ho.
22. "Models of Development Incorporating Income Distribution" (1972), 27 pp., James W. Land and Ronald Soligo.
23. "Disguised Unemployment in a Subsistence Economy" (1972), 19 pp., José Hamilton Gondim Silva.
24. "A Proposal for Research on 'Distribution of Gains, Wealth and Income from Economic and Political Development'" (1972), 67 pp., James W. Land.
25. "Optimal Wage and Education Policies with International Migration" (1972), 30 pp., R. Albert Berry and Ronald Soligo.
26. "Marketing and Economic Development: A Brazilian Case Study, 1930-70" (1972), 34 pp., Gordon W. Smith.
27. "Indigenisation of Industry and Progress of the Second Nigerian National Development Plan" (1972), 16 pp., Gaston V. Rimlinger.
28. "The Distribution of Incomes and the Short-run Burden of Taxes in Turkey, 1968" (1972), 38 pp., Marian Krzyzaniak and Süleyman Özmucur.
29. "The Proper Use of Indirect Taxation in Latin America: The Practice of Economic Marksmanship" (1972), 46 pp., Charles E. McLure, Jr.
30. "Distributional Equity, Inflation, and Efficiency in the Brazilian Fluctuating Exchange Rate System" (1972), 27 pp., Donald L. Huddle.
31. "A Diagrammatic Exposition of General Equilibrium Tax and Expenditure Incidence Analysis with One Immobile Factor" (1972), 36 pp., Charles E. McLure, Jr.
32. "Social and Economic Conditions and Political Violence" (1972), 26 pp., Fred R. von der Mehden with Kim Q. Hill.
33. "Income Distribution, Efficiency and the Experience of Colombian Farm Mechanization" (1972), 54 pp., Wayne R. Thirsk.
34. "Ease of Factor Substitution in Agriculture" (1972), 24 pp., Wayne R. Thirsk.
35. "The Contribution of Traditional and Small Scale Culture Goods in International Trade and in Employment" (1972), 26 pp., Yhi-Min Ho and Donald Huddle.
36. "The Distribution of Income and Tax Incidence in Panama, 1969" (1972), 39 pp., Charles E. McLure, Jr.
37. "General Equilibrium Incidence Analysis: The Harberger Model after Ten Years" (1972), 34 pp., Charles E. McLure, Jr.
38. "On the General Equilibrium Analysis of Tax Incidence" (1973), 34 pp., J. Gregory Ballentine and Ibrahim Eris.
39. "The Impact of Demand on Labor Absorption and the Distribution of Earnings: The Case of Brazil" (1973), 47 pp., Samuel A. Morley and Jeffrey G. Williamson.
40. "A Note on Z Goods, Marketed Surplus and the Labor Intensity of Small Farm Agriculture" (1973), 22 pp., Wayne R. Thirsk.
41. "The Incidence of Colombian Taxes, 1970" (1973), 66 pp., C. E. McLure, Jr.
42. "What to Do about Foreign Direct Investment: A Host Country Perspective" (1973), 28 pp., Samuel A. Morley.
43. "Income Distribution Consequences of Agricultural Price Supports in Colombia" (1973), 32 pp., Wayne R. Thirsk.

44. "Factor Intensity of Consumption Patterns, Income Distribution and Employment Growth in Pakistan" (1973), 34 pp., Ronald Soligo.
45. "Industrialization in Malaysia: A Penang Micro-Study" (1973), 42 pp., Fred R. von der Mehden.
46. "Short-run Effects of Income Distribution on Some Macro-economic Variables: The Case of Turkey" (1973), 33 pp., Tuncay M. Sunman.
47. "The Inequity of Taxing Iniquity: A Plea for Reduced Sumptuary Taxes in Developing Countries" (1973), 51 pp., C. E. McLure, Jr., and W. R. Thirsk.
48. "A Numerical Exposition of the Harberger Model of Tax and Expenditure Incidence" (1973), 51 pp., C. E. McLure, Jr., and W. R. Thirsk.
49. "Public Goods and Income Distribution: An Explanatory Comment" (1974), 17 pp., C. E. McLure, Jr.
50. "Education and Modernization in Zaire: A Case Study" (1974), 29 pp., Gaston V. Rimlinger.
51. "Rural Credit and Income Distribution in Colombia" (1974), 26 pp., Wayne R. Thirsk.
52. "The Short-run Burden of Taxes on the Turkish Agriculture in the Sixties," (1974), 41 pp., Marian Krzyzaniak and Süleyman Özmucur.
53. "Some Aspects of Efficiency and Income Distribution in Colombian Land Reform" (1974), 25 pp., Wayne R. Thirsk.
54. "Income Distribution and Colombian Rural Education" (1974), 23 pp., Wayne R. Thirsk.
55. "The Within-Nation Distribution of Public Expenditures and Services: A Two-Nation Analysis" (1974), 19 pp., Kim Q. Hill.
56. "Managerial Discretion and the Choice of Technology by Multinational Firms in Brazil" (1974), 37 pp., Samuel A. Morley and Gordon W. Smith.
57. "Inflation and the Share of Government Tax Revenue in National Income: An Empirical Test" (1974), 31 pp., Yhi-Min Ho.
58. "The Choice of Technology: Multinational Firms in Brazil" (1974), 42 pp., Samuel A. Morley and Gordon W. Smith.
59. "The Developmental Significance of the Rise of Populism in Colombia" (1975), 21 pp., Robert H. Dix.
60. "Inflationary Financing, Industrial Expansion and the Gains from Development in Brazil" (1975), 43 pp., Donald L. Huddle.
61. "Noneconomic Factors in the Study of Economic Development" (1975), 43 pp., Robert Cartier.
62. "Social Groups and Religious Values as Factors in Economic Development: A South Asian Example" (1975), 25 pp., Robert Cartier.
63. "The Bodpagaun Project: A Case of Economic Development" (1975), 29 pp., Robert Cartier.
64. "Some Economic and Political Characteristics of the Low-Income Housing Market in Bogotá, Colombia and Their Implications for Public Policy Alternatives" (1975), 36 pp., Timothy O. Gauhan.
65. "Public Expenditures and Services as Policy Outcome Predictors: A Two-Nation Analysis for Health and Education" (1975), 39 pp., Kim Quaile Hill.
66. "Low Income Housing Development in Bogotá (1975), 33 pp., Stephen O. Bender.

I

SOCIAL AND POLITICAL PROBLEMS

DECOLONIZATION AND INCOME DISTRIBUTION IN TROPICAL AFRICA

by Gaston V. Rimlinger

I. INTRODUCTION

The worldwide decolonization drive after World War II marked the end of the colonial system that had been forged largely in the late nineteenth-century scramble among the major European powers over the division of the African territory. Starting with the Gold Coast (Ghana) in 1957, new sovereign states emerged from artificial colonial jurisdictions in one area after another. There are now thirty-six black African countries, all but two (Liberia and Ethiopia) of which have become independent since 1957. The advent of independence in Africa naturally raised anticipations of great economic and social change. There were hopes and expectations that once the shackles of colonialism were removed, the new countries could mobilize productive energies that would lift the masses out of illiteracy and poverty. But informed observers had no illusions about the enormous development problems that lay ahead, some of which were legacies of the colonial economic system.

Although there was considerable variation in colonial practice, it had been marked everywhere by political, economic, racial, and social inequalities. Europeans from the metropolitan countries were naturally in the dominant positions; they occupied all of the well-paying jobs in government and private enterprises. Only in East Africa, mainly in Kenya, did Europeans play a major role as farmers and ranchers, and there they occupied the choice coffee-growing highlands. (We are not concerned in this essay with white-ruled South African countries.) In francophone West Africa, it was not uncommon to find French men and women, the so-called "petits blancs," in lesser economic positions in trade and the services. The middle economic and social layer, however, was generally occupied by non-European immigrants. In West Africa the Levantines (Lebanese, Syrians, Cypriots) and in East Africa the Asians (Indians and Pakistanis) controlled much of the trade, transport, and small industries. The overwhelming majority of the Africans were on the lowest rungs of the economic ladder.

Mr. Rimlinger is Professor of Economics at Rice University.

The Europeans used their dominant positions to keep the other groups in subordinate positions, notwithstanding the fact that European-run schools helped to educate a thin African elite. In many colonies Africans were legally prevented from occupying certain positions or engaging in economic pursuits that might compete with European interests. They were mainly relegated to peasant farming and unskilled labor. In spite of that, they often had to pay a disproportionate share of the tax burden, either in cash or through forced labor, and received far less than a proportionate share of government services.

Until the later years of the colonial era, colonial administrations did not seriously aim at the general development of their territories. Their concern with development was chiefly motivated by the desire to make the colonies generate enough income to meet administrative expenses. The economic and social infrastructure which the government financed was oriented toward support of a law-and-order type of administration and toward export-related agriculture and mining. The construction of internal means of transport, such as railroads, was mainly for the purpose of evacuating crops and minerals, whose production and/or marketing was under the control of business interests from the metropolitan countries. The newly independent countries have sought to reverse this pattern of external control and dependence with their ambitious development plans. In theory, at least, they have aimed at both economic development and equality. The Second National Development Plan (1970-1974) of Nigeria, for instance, includes in its objectives the creation of "a just and equalitarian society" and "a land of bright and full opportunities for all citizens."[1]

We are now in the middle of the second decade of independence for most African countries, and this may be an appropriate time to ask how much development has taken place and more specifically who has benefited from it. The main concern of this essay is with the second half of the question.

The issue of the distribution of the gains from development and modernization has received increasing attention in recent years from students of development. Most of the developing world has become painfully aware that after a quarter of a century of international developmental activity, the gap between rich and poor, both internationally and within countries, seems to be widening rather than narrowing. The African countries seem to follow the general pattern. A fundamental question which arises is whether the direction of change in the institutional framework inherited from colonial times tends to perpetuate or to eliminate gross economic inequality. No doubt a great deal of change has occurred, and many Africans have risen to positions of power and affluence. The question is, how much has the average African shared in the fruits of development? Unfortunately, there are only scattered data available on income distribution in Africa. Much of the argument, therefore, has to be inferred from participation or

TABLE 1

DEVELOPMENT LEVEL INDICATORS FOR SUB-SAHARAN AFRICAN COUNTRIES

	1970 per capita GDP at 1960 market prices (US dollars)	Percentage share of mfg. and crafts in 1970 GDP	Percentage of Enrollment among school-age children in primary and secondary schools	Percentage of illiterates (aged 15 and over)
WEST AFRICA				
Dahomey	88	7	20	95.4
Gambia	120	2	19	90.0
Ghana	172	17	52	75.0
Ivory Coast	221	13	40	80.0
Liberia	210	6	45	91.1
Mali	50	12	15	97.8
Mauritania	129	2	4	95.0
Niger	71	6	8	95.0
Nigeria	75	9	19	88.5
Senegal	171	16	23	90.0
Sierra Leone	165	6	19	90.0
Togo	147	12	37	95.0
Upper Volta	40	10	7	95.0
CENTRAL AFRICA				
Burundi	44	5	18	90.0
Cameroon	136	16	52	85.0
Congo P.R.	174	13	73	80.0
Chad	51	8	8	94.4
Gabon	460	7	78	88.0
Rwanda	47	4	40	90.0
Zaïre	100	19	54	83.5
EAST AFRICA				
Botswana	95	11	60	67.1
Ethiopia	62	11	8	95.0
Kenya	125	15	30	80.0
Lesotho	64	1	66	41.4
Madagascar	109	11	44	66.5
Malawi	57	14	23	77.9
Mauritius	224	18	66	38.4
Somalia	56	9	4	95.0
Swaziland	170	17	53	70.0
Tanzania	82	9	23	85.0
Uganda	98	6	33	74.9
Zambia	264	11	47	52.6

Source: *Survey of Economic Conditions in Africa, 1972,* Part I (New York: United Nations, 1973), Table 1, p. 9.

lack of participation in economic activities and from the likely impact of governmental policies.

The countries with which we are concerned had an estimated population of around two hundred and forty million people in 1970. Many of them are listed among the very poorest countries in the world today. Although most of them have experienced respectable economic growth rates since achieving independence, they have also had some of the world's highest rates of population growth. Table 1 indicates the general level of development reached in various sub-Saharan countries by 1970. In almost half of them the gross domestic product (GDP) per capita measured in 1960 U.S. dollars was $100 or less. In some of the really poor landlocked countries like Mali, Upper Volta, Chad, Rwanda, and Burundi, the per capita GDP was only on the order of $50. In only five of the countries did per capita GDP exceed $200, and in none did it reach as high as $500. It may also be noted that in about half the countries the share of manufacturing and crafts in GDP did not exceed 10%, and in none did it reach 20%. In about half of the countries 90% or more of the population aged fifteen and over is illiterate. Only two countries have achieved a literacy rate of better than 50% in this age group. In less than a third of the countries are even one-half of the school-age children attending school. These are indications that levels of development and income in sub-Saharan African are still extremely low and that even if there were no income inequalities the standard of living would be depressingly low. It is with an awareness of this situation that many African leaders have declared that the chief problem they face is development, not income distribution. They seem to think, rightly or wrongly, that tackling both development and economic equality at the same time might risk achieving neither.

II. THE AGRICULTURAL SECTOR

An important clue to the income distribution in present-day Africa may be obtained from the prevailing occupational structure. The majority of the African labor force continues to be employed in low productivity subsistence agriculture. Data for 1970 indicate that in the independent black African countries about three-fourths of the labor force was engaged in agriculture.[2] This high percentage of the work force, however, produced only one-third of the gross domestic product in these countries. In other words, the output per member of the work force in agriculture was only one-sixth of the output per member of the work force in the rest of the economy. These figures cannot be assumed to be very precise, since most countries have only rough approximations of the output of subsistence agriculture. Nevertheless, there can be no doubt that the differential in productivity gives a rough order of magnitude of the differential in incomes.

Per capita income in agriculture in all likelihood is on the order of one-sixth of per capita income in the rest of the economy.

There are obvious difficulties in generalizing about an area as vast as tropical Africa, but some of the important factors which affect the income distribution within the agricultural sector should be noted. First, there is the question of the extent to which an enterprise or household is engaged in commercial or in subsistence agriculture or pasturage. A second factor, which is related to the first, is the size and productivity of the land at its disposal. A third factor is government policy, including trade and industrialization policy, taxation, research aid, extension programs, transportation, and fertilizer subsidies. Government policies also have important implications for the distribution of income between the agricultural and non-agricultural sectors.

The distinction between commercial and subsistence agriculture in Africa can be made roughly on the basis of production for export and production for local consumption. Most of the agricultural work force is engaged in the production of food for local consumption, which does not enter into market channels. In the Ivory Coast, for instance, a country which has concentrated on the development of a diversified commercial agriculture, only 10% of the production of grains, roots, and tubers, the staple food crops, was marketed in 1965.[3] There are, of course, locally marketed crops (including food and industrial crops such as cotton and tobacco), but their total value generally remains small by comparison with that of the big export crops such as cacao, coffee, tea, peanuts, palm products, rubber, bananas, and pineapples. Although there are a few countries, especially in East Africa, where export-oriented plantations are important, most of the export crops are produced by African farmers and peasants on relatively small holdings. Many of these small holders produce only small quantities for export and spend most of their resources on the production of food for their own subsistence. As a general rule, we may assume that the more important the production of commercial crops, the higher the income. Not infrequently, however, peasants in subsistence agriculture may hire out as wage laborers to commercial farmers or to non-agricultural employers.

It is probably fair to generalize that in those countries where export agriculture has expanded rapidly, income distribution in the agricultural sector has become more unequal. This result follows more or less inevitably from the uneven commercialization of agriculture. Those areas which are best suited for commercial crops and which have best access to urban or export markets tend to get an increasingly large share of the total agricultural income. In West Africa this phenomenon tends to favor the coastal and forest zones over the more arid northern zones. In the Ivory Coast, for instance, the monetary income of a peasant in the *departement du Sud* is three times as high as that of a peasant in the *departement du Nord.*[4] In the Cameroon, per capita monetary income in the cocoa growing zone in the south is four times as high as in North Cameroon. One might assume that some of this differential is offset by non-monetary income, but this is not the case. In the Cameroon, non-monetary income is twice as high in the south as in the north.[5] Similar patterns exist within other coastal West African countries and between the coastal and the Sahelian countries. In general, the farther inland one goes, the lower the importance of commercial agriculture, and the lower the per capita income. Even in northern Nigeria, which is one of Africa's major commercial peanut growing areas, per capita income tends to be much lower than in the south.

The distribution of land ownership is not a major factor in income distribution in most African countries because of the widespread survival of communal ownership, with holdings allocated and periodically reallocated among families. Ethiopia, with its feudal land tenure system, and Kenya, with its white settlers, were important departures from the traditional pattern. Recent revolutionary reforms have abolished feudalism in Ethiopia and nationalized land ownership. Kenya has undergone a massive program of land registration and transfer of land ownership from European settlers to Africans. While this program has eliminated some of the colonial legacies of inequality of land ownership, it has but increased inequality among Africans. Kenyan agriculture now includes wealthy African plantation owners whose income is in the thousands of dollars, some medium-sized agricultural enterprises, and a broad mass of small holders and landless peasants whose income is $100 a year or less.[6] The top layer is described by Colin Leys as men who "were linked professionally, socially and economically to the foreign capitalist enclave, borrowing from foreign banks, having accounts with foreign equipment suppliers, holding directorships in foreign companies. Their farms were mostly run by salaried managers, in some cases Europeans." At the other end of the scale he finds " 'the peasant' masses, mostly now with freehold land titles, though with little access to capital, extension services or other inputs, and . . . a growing minority of landless laborers and squatters."[7] The Kenya experience illustrates a distribution pattern which often follows decolonization measures: the overall structure of income distribution is not changed much, but *nouveaux riches* Africans replace non-Africans in many of the privileged positions.

In most sub-Saharan countries government policies have resulted in distribution effects which favor the non-agricultural over the agricultural sector. In was noted earlier that during colonial times the African peasant often bore more than his share of the tax burden and received less than his share of government services. Decolonization has not relieved the agricultural sector from this unequal burden, even though in absolute terms some farmers and peasants may be better off. An important part of the tax burden is passed on to the farmers through government agricultural pricing policies and duties. The export of agricultural produce is usually handled by official marketing boards. They buy the crops from the peasants through licensed buying agents and sell them on the international market. Although these boards were originally established for the purpose of stabilizing agricultural prices and incomes, they eventually became instruments for taxing the peasants through low producer prices. The surplus exacted from the peasants was partly transferred to the government and partly absorbed by commercial middlemen. In countries like Nigeria and Ghana, the marketing boards helped to build up substantial foreign exchange and capital surpluses during the 1950s.[8]

A pattern was thus established during the closing years of the colonial era of extracting a surplus from the peasants. With the coming of independence the new African governments understandably looked to this source of revenue for financing their rapidly rising administrative and developmental expenditures. The result was an irresistible tendency to put a maximum tax burden on the peasants, since there have been few alternative comparable tax bases. In recent times Ghanaian cacao farmers have received less than one-third of the price for which their cacao sold on the world market.[9] Only in a country like Nigeria, where petroleum has become a major alternative source of taxable surplus, has the government been able and willing to relieve the peasants. The federal government in Nigeria has taken over the marketing boards from the states, raised the official producer prices, and eliminated export duties. It is not yet clear, however, to what extent the implicit gains were passed on to the producers and to what extent they were absorbed by the buying agents acting as middlemen. It is axiomatic that to the extent that more favorable prices are passed on to the producers, they will benefit mainly the export farmers, resulting in increased income inequality within the agricultural sector. On the other hand, subsistence peasants need suffer no decline in absolute income as a result of the change in price policy.

Another aspect of government policy that has worked against the agricultural sector in most African countries is the general pattern of heavily protected import substitution industrialization.[10] The tendency of this policy is to raise the price of manufactured goods in relation to agricultural produce to the detriment of those working the land. Similarly, the bulk of governmental overhead expenditure has been for the benefit of the nonagricultural sector. Almost everywhere expenditures on rural amenities, such as schools, hospitals, pipe-borne water, sanitation, roads, and electrification lag far behind similar expenditures for urban areas.

While this imbalance in government services has so far favored the nonagricultural sector, an increase in government spending on such items as rural roads, fertilizer, and agricultural research may well increase income inequality within the agricultural sector. The introduction of high yield varieties, which brings down the cost and eventually the price of agricultural produce, may help mainly the more enterprising commercial farmers who know how to take advantage of them; the largely subsistence peasant who markets only small quantities may be hurt by the lower price. He probably lacks the resources and the skills to grow the new varieties, which may require irrigation, fertilizers, and pesticides.

During the colonial era, most of the agricultural research and extension work was directed toward export crops. The benefits from this policy were reaped primarily by the overseas customers and international trading firms. Within Africa, the benefits, as noted earlier, went first to the marketing boards and middlemen and last to the export farmers. In recent years the research emphasis has shifted to the locally consumed food crops. The leadership of this effort is in the hands of organizations like the International Institute of Tropical Agriculture in Ibadan (Nigeria) and its affiliated governmental research stations in various countries. Although it is doubtful whether tropical staple food crops will see a "green revolution" of the kind associated with rice, wheat, and maize, there is reasonable hope for substantial yield improvements and protein enrichments. Such advances are essential to raise the African standards of nutrition and living, but in the short run they often entail increased income inequalities.

In addition to the factors enumerated above, there are historical circumstances which have contributed to regional income inequalities. This is notably the case in West Africa with regard to the differentials between the coastal and the inland areas. In most West African countries the southern zone came much more extensively under the influence of Christian missionaries, and was therefore exposed to Western education. The northern areas were converted to Islam at an early date and resisted the inroads of Christianity and western schooling. Often colonial administrations "protected" Islamic areas from Christian missionary inroads. Even where Koranic schools were established in the north, they did not go much beyond the teaching of Arabic and the Koran. Northerners were, therefore, less prepared than southerners to take advantage of economic opportunities arising from modernization. This legacy from colonial times has affected not only regional income distribution but also the distribution among ethnic groups. The uneven preparation of diverse ethnic groups to share in the income opportunities created by development underlies much of the tribal tension that is encountered in many African countries. Opportunities for advancement and unequal preparation have thus created sources of conflict between ethnic groups that previously had little contact or had harmonious relations.

III. THE NON-AGRICULTURAL SECTOR

So far I have discussed mainly those factors which tend to affect the distribution of income within the agricultural sector, which includes most of the so-called traditional sector of the African economies. I turn now to an examination of the non-agricultural sector, which covers most of the modern sector. I have noted earlier the basic fact that per capita income is much higher in the modern than in the traditional sector. As in the case of agriculture, however, there are strong tendencies working toward income inequality within the non-agricultural sector. The main factors which affect income distribution in this sector are industrialization, the growth of the modern service industries, governmental employment, urbanization, and Africanization.

The income distribution consequences of industrialization work mainly in favor of the enterprise owners, the resident foreign managers, and the foreign suppliers of equipment and parts. A secondary group of gainers is the relatively small number of indigenous people who gain employment in the new industries, especially at the managerial level. Because they are in a protected monopolistic position, these industries are able to pay relatively high wages. They are inclined to respond affirmatively to government or trade union pressures for higher wages and simply to pass on the higher costs to the consumers. Not only does such behavior redistribute income in favor of a minority employed in the monopolistic industries, but it locks the industries into a high-cost-high-price structure which greatly limits expansion and favors stagnation. Most governments are aware of these problems, but the situation is not one which can be easily altered.

The mining industries are another branch of the modern sector which expanded rapidly after World War II and particularly after independence. Independent sub-Saharan Africa produces substantial quantities of petroleum (Nigeria, Gabon), copper (Zaire, Zambia, Uganda), iron ore (Liberia, Mauritania, Sierra Leone, Swaziland, Guinea), bauxite (Guinea, Sierra Leone, Ghana), tin concentrates (Nigeria, Zaire, Rwanda), diamonds (Zaire, Ghana, Sierra Leone), gold (Ghana, Zaire, Ethiopia), and phosphate rock (Togo, Senegal). There are some small-scale locally operated mines, but most of the mining enterprises involve highly sophisticated technology and large capital investments and are normally undertakings of large multinational firms. Because the operating methods are not highly labor-intensive, they do not generate much employment. The distribution is thus weighted against returns to local labor, but in the case of the mineral industries the returns to the foreign firms are limited by the host countries' claims of rents, royalties, and profit taxes. How much the countries can claim depends, of course, on the profitability of the industry.

The outstanding case is the petroleum industry, from which government revenue in Nigeria increased from less than one billion dollars in 1971 to over seven billion in 1974. The distribution effects of this huge increase in revenue will depend heavily on the pattern of government spending and allocation to the states. The immediate effects in Nigeria seem to be working mainly in favor of the modern sector, particularly government employees, who have received substantial salary increases, averaging around 130% at the bottom of the scale and ranging from 70% to 100% at the top.[11] These awards, which were announced at the end of 1974 but made retroactive to April 1, 1974,[12] have unleashed tremendous pressures on the private sector to match the governmental pay increases. The result has been a serious acceleration of inflation, particularly of food prices, no doubt because rising costs of transport and handling reinforced an underlying trend of food production shortfalls in recent years. In all likelihood much of the recent increase in food prices will be absorbed by middlemen who control the means of transport and storage, with only a fraction passed on to the producers. Thus, while the immediate effects of the increased government revenue probably strongly favor those groups who are already the most privileged, this need not be the case in the long run. The new five-year plan (1975-1980) anticipates major expenditures for agriculture, rural development, and primary education, which should spread some of the benefits from the oil revenues to hitherto less favored groups. The allocation of federal revenue to the states has been made more equitable over the last year by greater attention to size of population and to need.

The most rapidly expanding sector of the African economies since independence has been the service sector, and in particular government employment. It is also this sector which until now has offered the best salaries, especially for the educated young Africans streaming in increasing numbers from universities. Data for several francophone countries, given in table 2, show that average monthly pay in the tertiary or service sector is between two and four times the level in the primary, mainly agricultural sector. Differentials between the secondary or industrial sector and services are less but still very substantial. Particularly noteworthy is the differential between private and public employment in the tertiary sector. High-level government employment has been the most important avenue for upward economic and social mobility in post-colonial Africa. Because of the drive to Africanize all the senior positions previously held by colonial administrators, there were unusual opportunities for rapid advancement in the early years of independence. The remuneration and benefit pattern that had been set by the colonial powers for their administrators was usually copied by the new countries, accounting in part for the high salary levels in relation to the rest of the economy.

Among the groups that were in the best position to profit from the economic opportunities presented by independence were naturally those who were educated. A stratified sample survey of incomes of 1635 heads of

TABLE 2

AVERAGE MONTHLY PAY
(in CFA francs)

	Ivory Coast 1971		Cameroon 1971		Madagascar 1965	
Sector	*private*	*public*	*private*	*public*	*private*	*public*
Primary	14,140	12,010	9,583	n. a.	4,413	4,816
Secondary	28,909	27,270	25,333	n. a.	8,347	6,263
Tertiary	39,430	50,235	26,583	n. a.	9,890	11,660

Source: Jacques Lecaillon and Dimitrios Germidis, "Les disparités de salaries au Sénégal, Cameroon, Madagascar, et Côte d'Ivoire," in *ILO World-Employment Research Working Paper,* tables IV-A, IV-D, IV-G, IV-K, mimeograph, 1974.

TABLE 3

AVERAGE INCOME OF HEADS OF HOUSEHOLDS
(in Relation to Level of Education in Nigeria in 1967)

Education	Annual Income (Nigerian pounds)
Illiterate	130
Primary	220
Secondary	351
University	1543

Source: O. Aboyade, *Incomes Profile,* (Ibadan: University of Ibadan, 1973), p. 19.

households in Nigeria in 1967, presented in table 3, reveals a particularly high return to university education (although the number of people in the sample with university degrees was rather small). The avenues for employment opened up by education are reflected also in the fact that 98% of the illiterates and 90% of those with only primary education were self-employed, whereas only 35% of those with secondary education and none of the seven people with university education were self-employed.

The Kenyan experience, although not necessarily representative, may nonetheless be taken as indicative for Africa as far as growth of employment opportunities in the public sector is concerned. Between 1964 and 1970 the number of Africans employed in the public sector grew by 66,000, while over the same period the corresponding increase in wage employment in modern private industry and commerce was only 21,000.[13] As is well known, it has been mainly the opportunities for wage employment which have attracted large numbers of laborers from the country to the city. The influx from the rural to the urban areas, however, has been much greater than the opportunities for employment. In Kenya, for instance, urban population has been growing at the rate of 10% per annum while recorded employment was growing at a rate of only 1.5%. Even though there were unrecorded employment opportunities in the so-called "informal sector," the problem of urban unemployment in Kenya is one of "appalling intensity and extent."[14] Estimates for Nairobi are that almost one-fourth of all adult males and over one-half of all adult females either are unemployed or lack the opportunity of earning a reasonable minimum income.[15]

Unemployment and very low earnings, often despite very long working hours, are major factors contributing to economic inequality in urban Africa. At the other end of the scale, a class of *nouveaux riches* is emerging in the rapidly growing African cities. Among them are the senior civil servants, senior military officers, executives and owners of large business establishments, and professional groups, especially lawyers. This class has access to finance and information, and to governmental permits and licenses. One source of rapid gains for them has been the skyrocketing real estate values in major cities like Lagos, Abidjan, and Nairobi. According to a recent estimate, land in central Lagos (Lagos Island) sells for around $600 a square yard, and office space rents for around $16 a square foot per annum. Modest accommodations on the Lagos mainland (Surulere) rent for around $5000 a year, but modern new houses on residential Victoria Island rent for around $30,000 a year, with rent paid five years in advance.[16] Clearly, only well-to-do Nigerians can share in this development bonanza. The masses are left behind. In Lagos, as in other major African cities, there are daily reminders of deep-seated inequalities in the contrasts between spacious modern dwellings and overcrowded native quarters, between air-conditioned supermarkets and unsanitary local markets, between those who ride in chauffeur-driven Mercedes-Benzes and those who sweat in "mammy-waggons."

There are indications that Africanization of assets and jobs may well tend to increase these inequalities. We have already noted that in Kenya Africanization of land ownership increased the wealth and income gap between rich and poor Africans. In other countries, policies with regard to Africanization of industry seem to have had similar effects. This is the judgment of a leading Nigerian scholar with regard to his country: "Rather than engender a redistribution of income, the indigenization policy will tend to concentrate a large amount of Nigeria's resources in the hands of a few highly placed, status-conscious and conspicuous-consumption-oriented class [sic] of Nigerians."[17] The note of disappointment in Professor Okediji's statement is widely shared among African intellectuals.

The most important feature of Nigeria's indigenization policy is contained in the 1972 Indigenization Decree, which required that by March 31, 1974, a group of twenty-two specified industries (mainly small-scale industry, transport, retail trade, and services) had to be completely owned by Nigerians, and in another group of thirty-three industries, Nigerian ownership had to be at least 40% of each company. Although some exceptions were granted and a number of companies simply folded, the law has largely been carried out. Lucrative opportunities were thus created for Nigerians to invest up to several hundred millions of dollars. As yet, no official report of the transfer has been made public, so that there is no direct evidence on the extent to which Nigerian ownership may have become concentrated. Disappointment has been created among unsatisfied would-be buyers, and suspicions have been aroused mostly by the secret nature of the transactions. The secrecy lends support to the suggestion "that companies were discouraged from going public so that some 'big shots' might buy them through private treaties."[18] The fact is that only twenty-four of some eight hundred affected enterprises offered shares to the public through the Lagos stock exchange.[19] Most enterprises were sold through private arrangements, no doubt mainly to people with access to large bank credits. One factor discouraging public sales was the very low prices of shares fixed by the Capital Issues Commission, which invariably resulted in price/earnings ratios below five and sometimes below one. Here was an opportunity for people with limited means to become small capitalists. With the exception of two companies, all public issues were heavily oversubscribed, from 300 to 800%. To assure wide distribution, the authorities rationed out the purchases among the applicants. In the end, however, less than .1% of the population benefited from this widely publicized exercise in decolonization.[20]

IV. CONCLUDING REMARKS

Even though the data presented in this paper are very impressionistic, there is no way one can avoid the general conclusion that after a decade and a half of independence, the distribution of wealth and income among indigenous people in tropical Africa has become more unequal. This is hardly a surprising result, given the necessarily uneven nature of the development process and the very elementary state of the continent's economic development. On the other hand, there are many indications that inequality between Africans and non-Africans has decreased, which was after all one of the changes sought by independence. In most cases it is probably also true that the increase in inequality among Africans is primarily the result of more at the top than less at the bottom of the economic scale. The rich are getting richer, but the poor are not necessarily poorer. There is no hard evidence to show that the new urban poor are worse off than the traditional rural poor, although the former are more vocal than the latter. At present, Tropical African societies are generally still open. As yet, there is no hardening of the structure of inequality. If there are serious political dangers in economic inequality, they mostly still lie ahead. If present trends continue, however, and if population keeps growing faster than the food supply and job opportunities, as has been the case in recent years, there is indeed cause for concern for the future welfare of the average African. Much more research is needed to get an accurate overall picture of the complex problems involved and to evaluate their implications.

NOTES

1. Federal Republic of Nigeria, *Second National Development Plan 1970-74* (Lagos: Government Printer, 1970), p. 32.

2. Economic Commission for Africa, *Survey of Economic Conditions in Africa, 1972*, Part I (New York: United Nations, 1973), p. 103.

3. Samir Amin, *Le développement du capitalisme en Côte d'Ivoire* (Paris: Editions de Minuit, 1967), p. 74.

4. République de Côte d'Ivoire, *Plan quinquenal de développement économique, social et culturel, 1971-75* (Abidjan: Ministère du Plan, 1971), p. 30.

5. Jacques Lecaillon and Dimitrios Germidis, "Les disparités de revenus entre travailleurs ruraux et salariés urbains," in *ILO World Employment Research Working Paper*, Table II-G, 1974 (mimeograph).

6. International Labour Office, *Employment, Incomes, and Equality: a Strategy for Increasing Productive Employment in Kenya* (Geneva: ILO, 1972), p. 72.

7. Colin Leys, *Underdevelopment in Kenya* (Berkeley and Los Angeles: University of California Press, 1974), p. 74.

8. On Nigeria, see Gerald K. Helleiner, *Peasant Agriculture, Government, and Economic Growth in Nigeria* (Homewood, Ill.: Irwin, 1966), chapters 6 and 7.

9. According to *West Africa* (February 17, 1975), the farmers receive £209 per ton while the world market price is £700.

10. This pattern concentrates on developing industries for the production of goods that were previously imported. It normally requires high tariff protection against competition from foreign-made goods.

11. Patrick Sanwo and Alan Rake, "Udoji: The Word that Triggered the Pay Struggle," *African Development* (March, 1975): 53.

12. *West Africa* (January 6, 1975): 1-2, 25.

13. International Labour Office, *Employment, Incomes, and Equality*, p. 93.

14. Ibid., p. 64.

15. Ibid., p. 63.

16. Alan Shelley, "Property Development," *African Development* (March, 1975): 65 and 67.

17. F. O. Okediji, "Indigenization Decree and Income Distribution: The Social Implications," *Quarterly Journal of Administration* **9**, No. 2 (January, 1975): 155.

18. Patrick Sanwo, "Indigenisation: How It Has Worked?" *African Development* (March, 1975): N36.

19. "Who Are Nigeria's New Rich?" *West Africa* (December 2, 1974): 1451.

20. Sanwo, "Indigenisation," p. N36.

THE POLITICS OF INCOME DISTRIBUTION IN COLOMBIA

by Robert H. Dix

I. INTRODUCTION

Governments and political parties differ in their approaches to development. Some stress economic growth under the leadership of an elite, while at the same time limiting as much as possible the broad distribution of economic and social rewards, and limiting political participation. These we may call the developmentalists. Others—revolutionaries comprising a counter-elite—would reconstruct society in the interests of a radical redistribution of income and political power, perhaps, but not necessarily, as a prerequisite for sustained economic growth. Still others, the pluralists, would more nearly balance considerations of economic growth and the distribution of income and other rewards by allowing the more or less free competition of elites and would-be elites.

A fourth approach to development partakes of features of all three of the above, yet melds them in a distinctive combination. This is populism, by which I mean a political movement characterized by the mobilization by (usually marginal) elites of a heterogeneous mass base, beyond or "above" existing attachments, and offering a new cross-sectional identity focusing on a leader, the nation, social justice, or typically all three. Populism thus combines the elite leadership of the developmentalist approach, the mobilizational and redistributive emphases of the revolutionaries, and the heterogeneity or coalitional aspect of pluralism. While not confined to Latin America, nor necessarily dominant there, populism is nonetheless a common, if little understood and often overlooked, approach to development in the region. In particular, it has been notably a more prevalent and more popular approach to development than has been the revolutionary one.

Since 1958 Colombian governments have exemplified, even archetypically, the developmentalist approach toward economic and social policy. They did so until 1974 under the aegis of a rather special political arrangement called the *Frente Nacional*. The *Frente* was a formalized coalition between

---

Mr. Dix is Professor of Political Science at Rice University.

Colombia's two historic, elite-dominated parties, the Conservative and the Liberal. For the sixteen years between 1958 and 1974 these two parties were to hold—by constitutional fiat—equal numbers of seats in legislative bodies and in appointive posts at all levels of government (including the cabinet). The presidency was to alternate every four years between members of the two parties. The purpose of such an arrangement was to bring to an end the earlier fraticidal warfare between adherents of the two "hereditary hatreds," and at the same time to forestall a recrudescence of the military dictatorship which in the years 1953-1957 had appeared to threaten the traditional hold of the civilian elites over the Colombian political system. A further objective, implicit but not incidental, was to promote the development of the country under the suzerainty of those same elites.[1]

To the surprise of some, the National Front survived for its proffered sixteen years with only slight formal modifications. Furthermore, despite at times significant opposition to the agreement from dissident factions of the two traditional parties, such oppositions hardly challenged the developmentalist stance of the *Frente Nacional.*

By the late 1960s, however, the *Alianza Nacional Popular* (ANAPO) of General Gustavo Rojas Pinilla, the man who had ruled as dictator 1953-1957, had begun to challenge the *Frente* more seriously, and on partially different grounds. For ANAPO attacked the *Frente* not only on the propriety of an institutionalized sharing of power between Colombia's parties, it also sought to appeal to Colombians apart from or "above" their historic partisan loyalties, and on the basis of appeals for social justice and identification with the person and previous regime of the erstwhile dictator.

Founded by Rojas (who had been permitted by the government to return from exile) and a handful of supporters in 1961, ANAPO first ran candidates (as a Conservative faction) in 1962. In subsequent elections it ran candidates under the Liberal label as well. It gained in strength until in 1970 its presidential candidate, General Rojas himself, won 39% of the vote and, in a multi-candidate race, almost the presidency. *Anapistas,* in fact, claimed that they had been fraudulently denied victory over the government's candidate.

Two aspects of the rise of ANAPO especially concern us in this paper. One is the meaning for Colombia of the rise of the first mass party giving priority to income redistribution over economic development "from above." The second is the significance of the fact that the principal political challenge to developmentalism has taken the form of populism rather than a more strictly class-oriented, Marxist and/or revolutionary movement, which in some political and academic quarters would seem to be the expectation. The implications indeed extend beyond Colombia to suggest some things concerning the nature of political development in Latin America generally.

I will first seek to marshal the empirical evidence to delineate the nature of Colombian populism, and especially to distinguish it from the developmentalist parties of the *Frente Nacional,* as well as from a strictly class-oriented revolutionary party. The evidence is of several kinds. The first encompasses the roots of ANAPO's support in the population and consists largely of a post-election (1970) survey conducted in Bogotá; both pre-electoral and post-electoral surveys, as well as a 1968 survey, carried out in Cali (Colombia's third largest city); and a study of voting by barrio in Bogotá and Medellín (Colombia's second city) based on aggregate data.[2]

I will then examine, more briefly, the social and political backgrounds of the ANAPO leadership, based in considerable part on the studies of congressional and party leadership carried out at the Universidad de los Andes in Bogotá.[3] A content analysis of party programs and the party press lends further support to the analysis. There will follow a brief examination of *Anapista* organization and campaign techniques, based both on the party's own documents and on interviews with *Anapista* officials.

Finally, since ANAPO is no longer wholly what it was in its heyday, either in its characteristics or in its dimensions, we need to examine the changes which have taken place since April 1970, when its candidate nearly won the presidency of Colombia.

Having presented the evidence relating to ANAPO as a political movement, I will conclude by seeking to draw out the developmental and theoretical implications of the analysis as they relate both to Colombia and, more broadly, to political development in Latin America.

II. ANAPO—ELECTORAL SUPPORT

ANAPO, and political movements like ANAPO, pose an initial paradox because, while they draw much of their support on the basis of class alignments within the electorate that were previously quite unfamiliar to the country's partisan politics, they also receive important backing from some of the most tradition-minded elements in the society. In Colombia's case this heterogeneity becomes clear from an analysis of the *Anapista* vote.

There is no question that in the country's largest cities the vote for president in 1970 was strongly polarized along class lines, with the have-nots voting in substantial numbers for ANAPO's candidate, General Rojas. Both surveys and aggregate data show that the vote for ANAPO consistently increases as one descends the social scale, and that some 60-65% of the lower class vote went to ANAPO, a percentage which apparently exceeds that of other Latin American countries with significant class voting such as Chile and Argentina, and is not far behind the percentage of the working class vote going to working class parties in such European countries as Sweden and Italy.[4]

This was a startling development for Colombia, with its two historic multiclass parties. It appeared that ANAPO had brought about a substantial shift, from a "vertical" to a "horizontal" axis of politics, at least in the large cities in the 1970 election.

Certain qualifications need at once to be made, however. In the first place, the available surveys and barrio-level studies only reflect the vote in Colombia's three largest cities, which contain only 20% or so of the nation's population.

Secondly, the real dividing line among the classes in their support for Rojas came not between the lower two classes and the others, but between the middle and lower-middle class, at least in the barrio analysis, where these categories were distinguished (see table 1).

TABLE 1
OFFICIAL VOTING RESULTS IN STRATIFIED BARRIOS, BOGOTÁ
(In percentages)

	Pastrana	Rojas	Betancur	Sourdis	Blank	Total
CLASS						
Upper	75.8	8.3	11.9	3.5	.4	100
Upper-middle	67.0	11.9	17.6	3.0	.5	100
Middle	56.4	19.5	20.9	2.4	.8	100
Lower-middle	35.5	50.0	13.0	.8	.7	100
Lower	27.8	62.7	8.3	.3	.8	100
Slum	11.8	84.0	3.0	0.0	1.2	100
TOTAL	40.8	44.6	12.6	1.2	.8	100

Source: Campos and McCamant, p. 60.

Put another way, Rojas received 50% of the vote in lower-middle class barrios, while his principal opponent—the candidate of the *Frente Nacional* coalition—got only 36%.

The authors of the 1970 Cali surveys further show, by means of a kind of causal modeling, that attitudes toward the performance of the *Frente Nacional* government were more strongly and directly correlated with the vote than were variables such as social class.[5] This suggests that, even in the large cities, ANAPO's 1970 vote may best be viewed as an expression of protest which crosscut social classes, even though ANAPO did appeal more to lower than to higher social strata.

It is further worth noting that ANAPO received disproportionate support in the large cities in 1970 from the 21-30 age group, with the numbers of this age group actually voting approximately doubling between 1968 and 1970.[6] Age, then, was a socio-economic variable other than class which helped to account for General Rojas's strong urban showing in 1970.

Finally, and perhaps most importantly as concerns ANAPO's large-city vote, one must note the distinction between the lower class in most Latin American countries, including Colombia, and the classic European working class. In Latin America the rate of urbanization considerably outpaces any concomitant availability of industrial employment, and, hence, the formation of a class-conscious proletariat in the European sense. Such a proletariat is the major component neither of the urban lower class in a country like Colombia, nor of the ANAPO vote. ANAPO did receive strong support from manual workers in 1970, according to the sample surveys. Workers were not very numerous in the samples, however, while those workers who were also union members in fact tended to favor other candidates. Among occupational groups, it was shopkeepers and salesmen, including petty tradesmen, as well as domestic servants, who were, proportionately, ANAPO's chief supporters.[7]

Evidence from elsewhere in Latin America further suggests that urban migrants, among whom Rojas showed disproportionate strength in 1970, tend to see themselves as representing individual, rather than group or class, mobility.[8] Similarly, surveys show a tendency of ANAPO supporters to view its program as providing direct and immediate benefits rather than longer-range structural reforms or changes.[9]

Thus, even while the 1970 vote for ANAPO in the largest cities polarized the electorate along class lines to a degree unprecedented in Colombia, there was much to suggest that class struggle was not necessarily implied. Furthermore, the available evidence concerning voting patterns *outside* the large cities indicates that ANAPO's roots are by no means entirely a product of urban malaise.

True, when the *municipios* of the country are ranked by size into six categories, ANAPO's vote proves to be greater in the largest cities, and there is a noticeable tendency for the average *Anapista* vote to decline as one moves from the larger communities to the smaller. But the latter tendency is neither very consistent category by category nor, in most elections, very great beyond the first category, especially if one takes into account the undoubtedly greater obstacles to opposition organization and anti-establishment voting in the smaller communities.[10] Only when one compares the vote in "very rural" *caseríos* and *corregimientos* with the corresponding department-wide vote does the disparity in *Anapista* strength become truly striking.[11] In fact, fully a third of ANAPO's votes in the presidential elections of 1966 and 1970—and almost a half in 1972—came from *municipios* defined as rural.[12]

Finally, it should be noted that more than half of the population of such major cities as Bogotá and Cali is of rural or small town origin,[13] while the 1970 Bogotá survey (though not the Cali surveys) showed that those who were born in towns of less than twenty thousand persons had a much greater tendency to vote for ANAPO than did those born in larger communities.[14]

Taken together, the foregoing data clearly demonstrate that ANAPO, as the major opposition to the *Frente Nacional* both in dimension and portent, was very far from being merely a product of discontent in Colombia's largest cities, and that even those who were urban in residence were not necessarily urban in their orientations toward politics.

Regional voting patterns further point up the fact that ANAPO's strongholds have included parts of the country that are not particularly urban or "modern." Of the eight (of twenty-two) departments giving 40% or more of their vote to Rojas in 1970, three were indeed those whose capitals were Colombia's three largest cities (Bogotá, Medellín, and Cali). By almost any indicator of development (urbanization, education, income, quality of housing, hospital beds per capita) these departments (plus Atlántico with its capital, Barranquilla) outranked the other Colombian departments, usually by some distance.[15]

The other five strong *Anapista* departments, however, including the only three to give Rojas more than 50% of their votes in 1970, were classified by Campos and McCamant as "extractive, high tenancy" departments.[16] This is perhaps something of a misnomer, for one of these, the department of Santander, has an important industrial sector centered around oil production and contains Colombia's fifth largest city (Bucaramanga); another (Boyacá) has a steel mill at Paz del Río. Still, for all five the (1964) portion of the labor force employed in agriculture was over 50% and for three of them more than 60%.[17]

Similarly, rank-order correlations at the departmental level, while they show a positive correlation of ANAPO's vote with such indicators of development as literacy (.42), show an even higher correlation with land tenancy (.65).[18] The correlation between religiosity and the vote for ANAPO is a modest .41; nevertheless, the strong ANAPO departments do tend to be high in religiosity (even while others that are high in religiosity are not strongly *Anapista*).[19]

The evidence is not wholly satisfactory, but it does seem to suggest that support for ANAPO among the Colombian electorate does not come solely from the more urban and highly developed areas (and not from all of these, as indicated by ANAPO's weakness in the country's fourth largest city, Barranquilla, on the Atlantic Coast), but also from traditionalist regions being penetrated by change, and by migrants from these areas.[20]

There is a final relevant question concerning the derivation of the ANAPO vote, namely, to which party did that vote go prior to the rise of the new party? First of all, especially in 1970, ANAPO drew previous abstainers to the polls—presumably including many of the least "modern" and least politically efficacious among the citizenry.[21] Secondly, although in 1970 in the large cities ANAPO drew relatively more heavily from the Liberals than from the Conservatives, the majority of ANAPO voters, both nationwide and over a number of elections, have tended to be erstwhile Conservatives, and hence somewhat more clerically-oriented and somewhat more rural in background than other Colombians. This is evident both from responses to the Bogotá and Cali surveys and from the fact that, during the days of the *Frente Nacional* when all candidates had by law to run either as Conservatives or as Liberals, *Anapista* candidates running under the Conservative label as a rule garnered more votes than did Liberal *Anapistas.*[22] It should also be noted in this connection that ANAPO began its electoral life as a Conservative faction, and that the two times General Rojas himself ran for president under the *Frente Nacional* (1962 and 1970), he ran as a Conservative.

In short, ANAPO's electoral support has derived in considerable part from voters who were previous supporters of the Conservative Party, the principal political bulwark of Colombian traditionalism.

The traditionalist elements of *Anapista* support are further illustrated by certain facts of a non-electoral nature. One of the most vociferous organizations backing General Rojas in 1970 was Patrianal, a reserve officers' association.[23] ANAPO congressmen also manifest a relatively high level of contact with the clergy, and are highest of all the political factions in the number of visits they receive from representatives of peasant groups.[24] Supportive groups conspicuously do not include many labor unions. Although ANAPO congressmen report extensive contact with labor union leaders, such contacts do not often include leaders of the major labor confederations, the Union of Colombian Workers (UTC) or the Confederation of Colombian Workers (CTC).[25] Unions, as organizations, seldom openly back ANAPO.

In summary, then, we have in ANAPO a political movement which in its support is more nearly class-based than any in Colombian history, and more nearly so than most in Latin America, but which is at the same time a broad, heterogeneous coalition including support from some of the more traditionalist redoubts of Colombian political life. Evidence for the latter proposition derives from the nature of those urban elements that disproportionately favor ANAPO; from the size of the communities from which ANAPO's support derives; from the nature of the regions outside the large cities where ANAPO has its principal strength; from the political derivation of the ANAPO vote; and from the identity of those organized groups with which ANAPO has close relationships.

III. ANAPO—LEADERSHIP, PROGRAM, AND ORGANIZATION

Examination of ANAPO's leadership, program, and organization bears out its characterization as a modern mass movement deeply penetrated by elements of traditionalism.

The social backgrounds of ANAPO congressmen show them to be high-status individuals with, however, slightly lower social standing on the average than congressmen of the various factions of the traditional parties.[26]

In general, *Anapista* leaders are probably best depicted as "marginal" members of the Colombian elite—not usually part of the real "Establishment" or members of elite organizations such as the Jockey Club, but at the same time not differing markedly in status from the elites of the traditional parties.

Of course, it might reasonably be expected from the Conservative political origins of the *Anapista* leaders that they would not represent a genuine counter-elite; and it seems indicative that recent defections from ANAPO, including that of one of Rojas's sons, have been largely in the direction of a return to the Conservative fold.

It is also suggestive of ANAPO's political character that during the years when General Rojas was president-dictator of Colombia, the regime showed greater hostility to the industrial than to the landed elite, which of course has been the bedrock of traditional Colombia.[27] Rojas, though not of elite origin, came from a family of small landowners in rural Boyacá.

A final datum of interest concerning *Anapista* leadership is that its representatives in Congress reported relatively fewer contacts with the major economic associations than did those of other parties—except with ACOPI, the Association of Small Industrialists.[28] The differences are not great, but are perhaps indicative of a pattern. The members of ACOPI, while of course having high social status vis à vis Colombian society as a whole, are marginal in power and prestige compared, say, to the industrialists who are members of the National Association of Manufacturers (ANDI).

The leadership of ANAPO, then, appears to constitute not a counter-elite having its origin in deprived social strata, but rather a marginal elite seeking fuller access to the status and material rewards of the system.

ANAPO's program meanwhile has also reflected the ambiguity of the movement and its populist nature.[29] The ideological and political platform of the party, the party press, and its campaign rhetoric make broad appeals to the "popular classes," and often make vitriolic attacks on the personnel, policies, and institutions of the developmentalist *Frente Nacional.* Verbal assaults on the overall system of privilege in Colombia abound, replete with such assertions as "ANAPO is the revolution." Policy goals in the socio-economic field are portrayed as "socialism á la colombiana," and include nationalization of oil and other mineral resources, as well as of imports and the Bank of the Republic. The party platform also calls for access to housing for all social classes, measures to stem inflation, and the like.

At the same time, there is little inclination to speak of society in terms of class divisions or the need for deep-seated structural change. Appeals are to "the people" and to "popular unity," rather than to particular classes or to the concept of class struggle. The approach to agrarian policy is indicative, as it often is with Latin American political parties and governments. There is virtually no talk of land redistribution. The stress is instead on the mistakes and maladministration of the governments of the *Frente Nacional* in carrying out the current agrarian reform program, and on the need to form cooperatives and to increase agricultural productivity.

When appeals are directed at specific groups, they are as often middle-status groups such as teachers and retired army officers as they are workers or peasants. Symptomatically, the earlier Rojas regime is praised for the relative absence of strikes.

ANAPO sees itself as flourishing amid the failure of both capitalism and Marxism, with some attendant emphasis on a "communitarian" ethic, on cooperatives, and on the co-management of factories by workers. Its "socialist" stance has often seemed to mean little more than state policies on behalf of the poor and the middle class, with the possible exception of the proposed nationalization of the above-mentioned enterprises. Judging by the behavior and pronouncements of ANAPO's congressional delegation, we find it quite possible that many *Anapistas* do not take too seriously a program "popular" even to this degree.

Finally, the party program has important traditionalist elements. Military terms and references are quite frequent, while the party refers to itself not only as socialist but also as nationalist and Christian. All in all, ANAPO's program—somewhat vague to begin with—is a mixture of populist and traditional appeals with only very modest proposals for fundamental structural change.

Organizationally, in the large urban areas, and especially in Bogotá, ANAPO was, at its peak, the most effective party in Colombia. In this, it resembled a modern mass party, complete with myriad ward- or *barrio*-level organizations, regular dues and carnets, mass rallies, more or less regular party communications media, a centralized command structure, and strict party discipline.[30] In rural areas, however, and in many departments, the relationship of the party to its members and followers appears more closely to reflect the traditional roles of patron and client. Relationships within the party hierarchy itself, even in urban areas, also have shown traces of traditional political styles.

Meanwhile ANAPO has always been dependent to an unusual degree, even considering the relatively personalistic factionalism of Colombian party politics, on the leadership and personalities of General Rojas and his daughter, María Eugenia, the party's candidate for president in 1974. The party media (including both press and radio) contain constant references to, and praise of, both. All command decisions, including the appointment and expulsion of party officers at the departmental level, emanate from the top leadership and are enforced hierarchically. There is little real collective decision-making in the party, and little pretense of it (distinguishing ANAPO from most European mass parties, for example). There is little, either, of the kind of elite collegiality which tends to govern the Liberal and Conservative parties, and little of their decentralization and diffuseness of organization. The role of the leader(s), characteristic of populism, has been paramount.

Therefore, while with regard to mass mobilization ANAPO was in its heyday the most modern party in Colombia, nationwide it bore a number of the organizational traits of Colombia's traditional parties. In the last analysis it has been very much the product of mobilization "from above" by a party leadership centered in a *caudillo* and his family and close associates.

IV. ANAPO—CHANGE AND DECLINE

ANAPO, of course, has not remained entirely what it was at its inception or in its years of early growth. Particularly after its near-victory in the presidential election of April 1970, and its formal founding as a party in June 1971, it has undergone changes—some quite obvious, others more subtle—which bear significantly both on a fully adequate interpretation of ANAPO's role under the *Frente Nacional* and on its future in post-1974 Colombian politics. Such changes do not negate what has already been said about ANAPO in the years of its electoral rise and organizational maturing, but they do introduce certain qualifications.

Data from a 1972 post-electoral survey carried out in Bogotá essentially replicate, although with diminished sharpness, the 1970 data concerning the socio-economic characteristics of the urban ANAPO electorate.[31] Ideologically, however, ANAPO has in recent years moved noticeably leftward. Comparing ANAPO's "Decalogue" of the 1970 campaign, for example, with María Eugenia's twelve-point platform of 1974, one sees a definite shift of emphasis, both in content and phraseology. Whereas three of the ten points of the "Decalogue" concerned governmental mechanisms and relations with the Church, these matters are not mentioned in the 1974 platform. Instead, there is talk of "the progressive nationalization of basic industries," and of "a profound, drastic, and massive agrarian reform," language that did not appear in 1970.[32]

The generational transfer of effective leadership of the party from General Rojas to his daughter—who was always closer to the urban mass base of the *Anapista* electorate than was her father—partly accounts for such changes, as does the entry into the party of intellectuals from other political homes who were seeking in ANAPO a viable alternative to the traditional parties. Partly, though, the apparent change has evidently been a matter of tactics, with ANAPO leaders interpreting the 1972 fall-off in their vote as meaning that ANAPO had to take a stronger class-oriented line in order to make up for the partisan factional vote that had once accrued to it under the restricted competitive conditions of the *Frente Nacional.*[33]

As for ANAPO's leadership and organization, María Eugenia had increasingly become the real leader of the party well before her father's death in January 1975. In fact, by the early 1970s Rojas had come to play a largely symbolic and legitimizing role, seldom in direct contact with the party organization. A number of ANAPO's founders and early adherents (although by no means all) had left the ranks, as had some of the Liberals who had joined in the late 1960s. By the accounts of most observers, the party's membership and its grass-roots organization had both fallen well below the peak of 1970.[34]

Most notably, the party has experienced a marked decline in its electoral fortunes. Having captured 38.7% of the popular vote for president in 1970, its candidates won only 18.8% in the 1972 elections for departmental assemblymen, and a mere 9.4% in the 1974 presidential race.[35]

What accounts for the fall-off in the *Anapista* vote? The explanation is in the main speculative, but surely includes the following reasons:

1) It seems plausible that the constitution of ANAPO as a third party in 1971 and the approaching end of the National Front's enforced bipartisanship, heralded by the open competition for departmental legislatures and municipal councils in 1972, led many erstwhile Liberals and Conservatives to return to their ancestral partisan homes.

2) The tendency toward radicalization of the party, the more explicitly socialist proposals and class-oriented rhetoric of the 1974 campaign, may have alienated voters,[36] just as it drove from the party some of its long-standing loyalists among the leadership, especially in its former Conservative wing. By more clearly defining its programs, ANAPO may well have lost some of its ability to be all things to all men. Moreover, in choosing to make ANAPO somewhat more explicitly class-oriented, the party's leadership may have misinterpreted the new competitive situation and underestimated the historic pulls on Colombia's voters of the country's traditional multiclass parties.[37]

3) The disappointing performance of those *Anapistas* elected in 1970, not only in Congress but also in departmental assemblies and municipal councils, where they often held a majority, should also be noted.[38] There is

little evidence that in any of these legislative bodies *Anapistas* put forward specific programs for the alleviation of the immediate concerns of their constituents. Political bickering, sometimes among *Anapistas* themselves, and an alleged unseemly appetite for positions and perquisites, may have discouraged the party's followers who, by the very nature of their followership, expected instant redress for grievances which no party, in any event, could accomplish in short order.

4) The denial of victory legitimately won in 1970—at least as Rojas's supporters saw it—may, too, have played an important role in the downturn in ANAPO's subsequent electoral fortunes. In a post-electoral survey conducted in 1974 in Bogotá, many former ANAPO voters gave this (that is, the expectation that their candidate would be denied office even if victorious) as the principal reason for not voting for María Eugenia.[39]

5) In 1974 the fact that the *Anapista* candidate was a woman may also have hurt the party. It was the second most common rationale for their failure to vote for ANAPO given by former ANAPO supporters among the respondents to the 1974 Bogotá survey.[40] María Eugenia's candidacy may also have caused the disaffection of some of the party's more traditionalist leaders.

6) Finally, it seems probable that the peak attained by ANAPO in 1970 was itself a product of some exceptional circumstances. The vote for Rojas was in considerable part a protest against the *Frente Nacional* and its works, which had had their quintessential embodiment in the outgoing administration of Carlos Lleras Restrepo. The purported emphasis by the Lleras government on "development" at the expense of "social justice," on "technical" as opposed to "human" solutions, fueled the protest, as did scandals in some government agencies. During the course of the campaign, moreover, ANAPO—assisted by the denunciations of spokesmen for the *Frente Nacional*[41]—became identified as the principal focus of opposition to the Front. Perhaps even more important, Liberal voters had no Liberal for whom to cast their ballots in 1970. Many apparently turned to the "populist" Rojas, returning to the fold to vote for a Liberal president in 1974.

In sum, during the last year or two of the National Front, ANAPO became somewhat more coherently organized in an ideological sense, and more socialist-oriented, and to that extent less vaguely populist. There was also some change in its leadership and organization. At the same time, and most strikingly, it lost much of its earlier support, although as noted this may have been as much the cause of ideological change as vice versa.

Immediately following its 1974 debacle, ANAPO announced long-range plans for improving and expanding its radio outlets, for making *Alerta* into a daily paper, and for the more effective participation of workers, peasants, and other groups in the life of the party. It claimed that it had attained the important goal of establishing itself as a viable third party in free competition with Conservatives and Liberals.[42] Yet ANAPO was clearly badly demoralized, with deep-seated fissures showing between traditionalist and leftist elements in the party.[43] With its original *caudillo* dead, its future remained highly uncertain.

V. CONCLUSION

The nature of its organization, as well as aspects of its program and leadership composition, strongly suggest that ANAPO never really constituted a genuine counter-elite, despite its electoral base among the lower social strata of Colombian cities. Rather, it more nearly comprised a movement of dissident or marginal members of the elite manipulating the masses in the *name* of social justice, but essentially to promote their own political/economic advance.

Put another way, ANAPO has represented the political protest of those among both elites and masses who see economic development proceeding without full benefits or full participation accruing to them. It is both led and supported, however, by those who, by and large, see roles for themselves within the (albeit possibly modified) system, rather than by those seeking real structural change. It has indeed—for example, in the largely Conservative origins of its top leaders and the tendency of some of them to return to the fold of the mother party—certain of the attributes of a faction of one of Colombia's traditional parties. In fact, ANAPO has had a good deal of the negative protest movement about it, conjoining a number of disparate groups and political tendencies which for varying reasons opposed the political arrangements or the developmentalist policies of the *Frente Nacional.*

ANAPO is, then, not really opposed to the existing socio-political structure nor is it really a revolutionary party. At the same time, by its appeal to "the people," against the "oligarchs" and across traditional party lines, as well as in its political loyalty to a former military dictator, it has carried at least an implicit threat, not just to the personnel, policies, or mechanics of the *Frente Nacional,* but also to many of the fundamental political and social assumptions of the Colombian system.

Most important for Colombia's developmental future, ANAPO has been instrumental in fostering a partial tilt in the axis of socio-political conflict from an essentially vertical one (between multiclass parties) *in the direction of* a horizontal, class-defined axis, especially, though not exclusively, in the realm of voting behavior. Even should ANAPO fade as a political movement in the later 1970s, it seems unlikely that over the long term partisan competition in Colombia will wholly revert to its previous virtually non-class nature.

Yet while its mass, lower-class dimension has perhaps been ANAPO's most striking and important feature, to characterize it as a genuine class-oriented or revolutionary party omits or distorts significant aspects of its life as a political movement.

Rather, we have in ANAPO what I have called populism, or what Gino Germani has referred to as a "national popular" movement which seems "to represent the peculiar form of intervention of the traditional strata in the national political process in the course of rapid mobilization in countries of delayed industrialization."[44]

What stands out is the ambivalence and ambiguity of such movements, seeking as they do immediate benefits, including upward economic, social, and political mobility for their leaders, and welfare, public works, and entry into the consumer society for their followers, without paying the presumed cost of genuine development by real structural or attitudinal change. A desire for the rewards of development coincides with a kind of resistance to it, or to certain of its aspects or consequences.

There is a tendency for particular populist movements to be short-lived, because of their own internal contradictions and their frequent dependence on a certain leader or given set of circumstances.[45] But this *type* of movement can be expected to recur—in Colombia and in many other parts of Latin America—as a consequence of the persistence of the fundamental conditions that foster it.

It could, in fact, be argued that populism is the most "natural" type of mass movement for the sort of corporatist societies depicted by Philippe Schmitter as especially characteristic of contemporary Latin American politics. Such societies are rooted in late or delayed development, in which rapid urbanization far outpaces the growth of industrialization and an industrial proletariat, and where mass mobilization is controlled "from above" by governments, parties, and elites. Some of these aspects of late development are in turn reinforced by Hispanic political culture (e.g., in their corporatist aspects) and by external dependency.[46] In Colombia's case, its long heritage of popular loyalty to vertically-structured parties may enhance its susceptibility to mass mobilization by traditional elites.

Thus, in Colombia and in countries like Colombia, especially in Latin America, populist parties and movements like ANAPO tend to be more significant than strictly class-oriented, Marxist, and/or revolutionary parties, as political responses to the advent of mass suffrage amid the strains and prospects of the early-to-middle stages of the industrial revolution.

More often than revolutionary change under the aegis of a counter-elite, and at least as common as a pluralistic approach, populism, in the guise of marginal elites mobilizing a heterogeneous mass and unified around a leader, is the typical Latin American reaction to developmentalism. It is perhaps not a coincidence that, when in 1974 ANAPO sought to give its program a more explicitly class-oriented and revolutionary cast, it suffered a marked decline in its fortunes.

NOTES

1. Robert H. Dix, *Colombia: The Political Dimensions of Change,* (New Haven: Yale University Press, 1967), ch. 6.

2. All of these studies were published by Colombia's Departamento Administrativo Nacional de Estadística (DANE) in *Colombia Politica* (Bogotá, 1972). One of the studies appearing in the DANE volume has also been published in English, in somewhat revised form, as Judith Talbot Campos and John F. McCamant, *Cleavage Shift in Colombia: Analysis of the 1970 Election* (Beverly Hills: Sage, 1972). Where similar material appears in both, the English version has been cited, as Campos and McCamant. The DANE publication also includes considerable electoral data, principally for the years 1958-1970, and throughout has been used as the source for such data unless otherwise indicated.

3. Publications so far stemming from this project include Gary Hoskin, Francisco Leal, Dora Rothlisberger, and Harvey Kline, *El Comportamiento Legislativo en Colombia* (Bogotá: Editorial Universidad de los Andes, 1974); and Harvey F. Kline, "Interest Groups in the Colombian Congress: Group Behavior in a Centralized, Patrimonial Political System," forthcoming.

4. Campos and McCamant, pp. 8-9.

5. Ibid., pp. 72-74.

6. Ibid., pp. 56-57.

7. Rodrigo Losada and Miles Williams, "Análisis de la votación presidencial en Bogotá, 1970," in *Colombia Política.*

8. Alejandro Portes, "Urbanization and Politics in Latin America," *Social Science Quarterly* **52** (December 1971): 697-720.

9. Losada and Williams, "Análisis de la votación presidencial," pp. 28-29.

10. See, e.g., Daniel Premo, *Alianza Nacional Popular: Populism and the Politics of Social Class in Colombia, 1961-1970* (unpublished Ph.D. dissertation, University of Texas at Austin, 1972), pp. 105 and 344.

11. Lars Schoultz, "Urbanization and Changing Voting Patterns: Colombia, 1946-1970," *Political Science Quarterly* **87**, no. 1 (March 1972): 40.

12. Ibid., table 5, p. 39.

13. Ibid., p. 30.

14. Campos and McCamant, p. 59.

15. See, e.g., table 6, p. 85, in Fernando Uricoechea, *Modernización y Desarrollo en Colombia 1951-1964* (Bogotá: Universidad Nacional, Departamento de Sociología, 1967). I am also indebted to Professor Wayne Thirsk of the University of Manitoba, Winnipeg, Canada, for data made available to me.

16. Campos and McCamant, p. 53.

17. Data provided by Professor Thirsk. One of the departments, César, was formed subsequent to 1964 from some of the more rural parts of the department of Magdalena. The latter in 1964 had 61% of its labor force in agriculture.

18. Campos and McCamant, p. 51. Most such correlations, of somewhat dubious value at a level such as the departmental, tend in any case to be weak due to the diversity of ANAPO's support, thus tending to confirm one of my central points.

19. For data on religiosity (as measured by priestly vocation per capita), see Gustavo Pérez, *El Problema Sacerdotal en Colombia* (Bogotá: Centro de Investigaciones Sociales, 1962), p. 66. Four of the five departments which are highest in religiosity are among those most strongly *Anapista*. The correlation is with the 1966 vote for ANAPO.

20. A commercial city, Barranquilla (and the Atlantic Coast region in general), has always been one of independent Colombia's least traditional areas as judged by social customs, family patterns, religiosity, and so forth. Moreover, because of its distance from the more traditional departments, it has received fewer migrants from such areas.

21. Campos and McCamant, p. 101.

22. Losada and Williams, "Análisis de la votación presidencial," pp. 111-112.

23. Campos and McCamant, p. 39.

24. Kline, "Interest Groups in the Colombian Congress," p. 7.

25. Ibid., pp. 7, 10, and 18.

26. Hoskin, et al., *El Comportamiento Legislativo en Colombia.*

27. Albert O. Hirschman, *Journeys Toward Progress* (Garden City, N.Y.: Doubleday Anchor, 1965), p. 170.

28. Kline, "Interest Groups in the Colombian Congress," p. 18.

29. The analysis that follows was based primarily on the *Plataforma Ideológica y Política de Alianza Nacional Popular* of 1971, and on selected issues (1969-1972) of the principal ANAPO press organ, *Alerta.*

30. *Plataforma Ideológica . . . 1971*, pp. 62-64.

31. Rodrigo Losada and Gabriel Murillo, *Análisis de las Elecciones de 1972 en Bogotá* (Bogotá: Universidad de los Andes, Departamento de Ciencia Política, 1973), especially pp. 164-171.

32. For the text of the Decalogue see Saturnino Sepúlveda Niño, *Élites Colombianos en Crisis* (Bogotá, 1970), pp. 74-77; the 1974 platform was published in a pamphlet entitled *Bases de una Nueva Colombia.*

33. See *El Espectador,* (Bogotá), April 24, 1972, p. 2A.

34. An ANAPO official admitted a 25% diminution in an interview, Bogotá, July 23, 1974.

35. The above calculations were based on data from Registraduría Nacional del Estado Civil, *Estadísticas Electorales: 1972* (Bogotá, 1972) and from preliminary 1974 figures provided the author by the Registraduría.

36. There is little direct evidence to support this interpretation, however. The decline in the 1974 vote for ANAPO was proportionate in urban and rural areas.

37. Rojas's son-in-law saw the 1970 elections as portending a class struggle, despite what he claimed were ANAPO's efforts to prevent it; *Revista Javeriana* **73**, no. 365 (June 1970): 529-538.

38. For María Eugenia's reply to such charges ("we are being slandered") see *El Siglo* (Bogotá), Feb. 21, 1972, p. 6.

39. Gabriel Murillo, interview, Bogotá, July 24, 1974. This coincides with the attitudes of *Anapistas* expressed in the wake of the 1970 election that they had been denied their rightful victory. See Campos and McCamant, pp. 68-69.

40. Gabriel Murillo, interview, July 24, 1974. On the other hand, 73% of the respondents in the 1972 Bogotá survey indicated that being a woman was no obstacle to becoming president of Colombia: Losada and Murillo, p. 217.

41. The Bogotá newspaper, *El Tiempo,* led in this respect; cf. Premo, *Alianza Nacional Popular,* p. 344.

42. *Alerta,* April 24, 1974, pp. 3, 4, and 5.

43. A high ANAPO official asserted following the 1974 election that María Eugenia was at the center of the party ideologically, and that she was a political pragmatist who would move ANAPO in whichever direction political survival seemed to indicate; interview, Bogotá, July 23, 1974.

44. Gino Germani, *Política y Sociedad en una Epoca de Transición* (Buenos Aires: Editorial Paidos, 1965), p. 157.

45. The movement headed by Carlos Ibáñez del Campo in Chile (1952-1958) is a classic example of the frequently ephemeral nature of such movements; that of Getulio Vargas in Brazil is more ambiguously so. The Peronist movement in Argentina has of course been something of an exception.

46. Philippe Schmitter, "Paths to Political Development in Latin America," in *Changing Latin America,* ed. Douglas A. Chalmers (New York: Columbia University, The Academy of Political Science, 1972), pp. 83-105.

INTEREST GROUPS AND GOVERNMENT POLICY IN MALAYSIA

by Fred R. von der Mehden

The traditional manner of analyzing the functions of organized private interest groups in modern democratic systems has primarily centered upon an assessment of the efforts of organizations to influence the input functions of government, i.e., to study the means by which various types of pressure groups attempt to create an impact upon voters, legislators, the executive branch and, in some cases, the judiciary. Analysis has concentrated upon methods of influencing the formulation of laws and regulations whose effect might be to aid or injure the organization involved. In this study of the interaction between the public and private sectors in Malaysia, I seek to analyze the extent to which this pattern of influence is also present in a developing democratic system. It is the contention of this paper that, in fact, the Malaysian firm or organization is primarily interested in influencing the output rather than the input functions of government; i.e., it seeks to decide how laws and regulations already formulated shall affect the organization. Thus, influence is directed more at the implementation of laws and rules by the administrative elements of government. In an effort to elucidate this practice, the study will investigate types of contacts between government and the private sector, attitudes of the private sector towards government, and methods of influence. The focus will be primarily upon the industrialization and development policies of the Malaysian government, both programs with income re-distribution goals.

Malaysia provides an interesting comparison with western democratic states. It is one of the few Afro-Asian countries with competitive political parties, a working parliamentary system, and public support of both Western and national entrepreneurial activities. A pluralist society, Malaysia accepts economic and political activities by private organizations within certain constitutional limits. Thus there exist functional interest groups representing various economic and social activities: tin and rubber producers, Chinese and Indian chambers of commerce, and educational organizations, as well as private firms. Like the United States, but unlike many of its Asian neigh-

Mr. von der Mehden is Albert Thomas Professor of Political Science at Rice University.

bors, Malaysia does not have functional group representation as such in its legislature. Although official interest groups, particularly parties and the civil service, have a prominent part in the political system, this paper will concentrate on private organizations.

METHOD

The basic assertions made in this paper have been derived from two surveys carried out in Malaysia during 1973. The first was of two hundred twenty-eight of the thousand largest companies in West Malaysia and seventeen associations (such as chambers of commerce) throughout West Malaysia. In 82% of the encounters, a top-level man in the organization was interviewed. The sample was selected to reflect geographic distribution (somewhat weighted in order to obtain representation from the entire peninsula), ownership (local, foreign, and joint enterprises), race of owner, and types of businesses (associations, processing of primary products, western trading companies, Asian trading companies, food manufacturing, engineering, other manufacturing, service industries, and financial institutions).[1] The survey had a high proportion of open-end questions, which were coded after field work was completed. The survey sought answers on sources of information on government policies, type and frequency of contact with various elements of government, awareness and attitudes toward Malaysian government economic policies (with particular emphasis upon the New Economic Policy[2]), and problems in dealing with government.

The second survey was of thirty-six firms in two industrial estates and one Free Trade Zone in Penang. This was an in-depth survey carried out with the aid of students from the Universiti Sains Malaysia, and it incorporated firm histories. Managers or owners and a sample of workers were interviewed to assess their experiences in the development of new industrial enterprises or the expansion of old ones. Two general lines of questioning were the focus of this survey: 1) the experiences of regionally based firms with government, and 2) the extent to which the industrial development program in Penang related to the overall Malaysian plan to eradicate poverty and raise the standards of the Malays through the NEP. Beyond these two surveys analysis was also made of membership of boards of companies and the history of industrial development in Malaysia; additional interviewing took place in 1974-75. The research design was developed to provide economic and social analysts in the Rice University Income Distribution Program with the political bases for decision-making on economic policies in Malaysia.

Interviews in both cases were carried out by university students trained and supervised by the author and/or a commercial survey firm. Considerable care was taken to allay suspicions of firms, and prior to interviews managers were informed by letter as to the nature of the study and the anonymity of their answers. A high percentage agreed to participate although local Chinese were less willing than other managers to be involved. Interviews were given in the language of the respondent and generally lasted fifty minutes in the national sample. The Penang study respondents were often interviewed several times over a four week period.

INFORMATION FOR DECISION-MAKING

In order that groups be able to influence policy, it is necessary that they have access to data on government policies and regulations, and the ability and desire to employ that information. A very high percentage (87%) of firms interviewed noted that they kept informed of national government matters. On close scrutiny, however, a pattern can be discerned which was mirrored throughout the interviews. Knowledge and use of information about government programs in Malaysia are weighted in favor of firms characterized by non-Chinese, foreign, or joint venture ownership, and by residence around the capital city state of Selangor. While variations are not great, they do display significant geographic and ownership biases, particularly if such attempts to keep informed were regular.

TABLE 1

MANAGEMENT INFORMED OF FEDERAL GOVERNMENT MATTERS

(In percentages)

	Ownership Local	Foreign	Joint	Selangor	Rest W. Malaysia	Chinese	Others
Do keep informed	83	90	95	91	83	82	97
Do not keep informed	17	10	5	9	17	18	3
Informed on regular basis	68	81	89	79	70	65	92
Informed irregularly	15	10	6	12	13	16	5

A much higher percentage of managers in firms with foreign ownership was involved in gathering and maintaining knowledge than the percentage of managers in locally owned firms, underlining the importance to such businesses of regular information.

Part of the explanation for these variations was to be found in geographic location, the language difficulties, and the character of the firm. Those outside the capital found it less easy to maintain regular access to the national government, but it should be noted that firms in the distant East Coast states were better informed on state matters than those in Selangor. Chinese firms reported finding it difficult because of the language barrier to understand government publications written in Malay or English or to discuss issues with officials. Finally, the character of the firms is an important variable. Foreign multi-nationals or agency houses have developed long experience in gathering commercial data, and joint venture firms have often been closely tied to government programs or have been formed under official auspices. The Chinese firm has traditionally believed it to be wise to stay clear of government except when necessary. It has depended upon its associations or third parties rather than officials. This attitude is changing, and Penang Chinese respondents reported a desire to gain better access to government, but were hobbled by lack of knowledge as to points of contact.

PERSONAL CONTACT

While we have noted the high degree of interest in data among large firms in Malaysia, the traditional picture of influence in Asia has been personal contact between businessmen and officials. It is here that we begin to see the evidence against the hypothesis that in Malaysia the interest group primarily attempts to influence the input functions of government. In the national survey of large firms, contacts with two types of government officials were investigated: 1) non-civil service, and 2) civil service or members of quasi-government authorities. The former would be considered those approached as political contacts, including federal and state ministers, members of parliament, ambassadors, or royalty. Slightly less than 50% of almost all categories had contact with this group, most notably with ministers, MPs, and state representatives (table 2). Interestingly, although foreign firms maintained closer touch with published data, they were significantly less

TABLE 2
CONTACT WITH NON-CIVIL SERVICE MEMBERS OF GOVERNMENT
(In percentages)

	Total Firms	Associations	Local	Foreign	Joint	Chinese	Other	Selangor	Rest
Have contact	45	71	49	32	48	46	47	40	52
Do not have contact	55	29	51	68	52	54	53	60	48

involved in political contacts. While the total percentage of firms with such contacts was 45% and associations displayed a high 71%, only 32% of foreign firms admitted to relationships of this kind. In this we can see a caution, probably combined with a lack of experience, in dealing with political figures in Malaysia. In any case, they were consistently less likely to deal with ministers, MPs, and state representatives informally than were other groups (no foreign firm would admit to informal entertaining of those specifically described as "politicians"). The type of interaction with MPs and senators, for example, was primarily through direct formal contact or letter (averaging 20% of all respondents) and informal entertainment (averaging 12% of all firms, but ranging from 6% for foreign firms to 15% for joint venture firms). Informal entertainment was the most notable means of contact with state representatives, but averaged 12% (from 3% with foreign firms to 14% for local firms). No category of those surveyed stated that contact with non-civil servants was very frequent, the majority saying it was less than once in six months.[3]

Thus the data from this survey showed low contact with those political leaders responsible for the promulgation of laws and regulations. Less than 25% of the firms or associations admitted to contact with MPs, for example. Several firms had MPs on their boards of directors, but the usual comment was that they had not proved "useful." While we may question the veracity of some of the answers, they do tend to validate the point that comparatively little public effort is made to influence the input functions of government in Malaysia.

If, as we hypothesize, primary emphasis is on influencing the output functions of government, then contacts with civil servants and members of quasi-government authorities would be much higher. Care should be taken to avoid extrapolating too much from the figures that follow, since doing business in most countries entails frequent contact with government functionaries with regard to licenses, taxes, permits, etc. Still approximately twice as many firms reported contacts with civil servants and quasi-government officers as with political authorities.

TABLE 3

CONTACT WITH THE CIVIL SERVICE AND QUASI-GOVERNMENTAL AUTHORITIES
(In percentages)

	Total Firms	Associations	Local	Foreign	Joint	Chinese	Other	Selangor	Rest
Have contact	93	93	93	94	94	92	95	93	94
Do not have contact	7	7	7	6	6	8	5	7	6

As can be seen from table 3, there was little variation among types of firms in the sample. Among firms in the Penang sample with fewer workers, a significantly smaller number of Chinese firms reported contact with civil servants, but the pattern was more a question of frequency of contact. Not only was there a more general reporting of contact with civil servants in the total sample, but also such contact was considerably more frequent than contact with politically-oriented individuals.

COOPERATION WITH OTHER COMPANIES

A final and important area of contact for those interested in influencing government is joint action among firms with common interests. This can be particularly effective in affecting the input functions of government, as can be seen in the United States through the National Association of Manufacturers, commodity associations, professional groups, and so forth. This was not a common practice in Malaysia, where less than a quarter of the firms reported such activities (see table 4).

TABLE 4
COOPERATION WITH OTHER COMPANIES ON GOVERNMENT MATTERS
(In percentages)

	Total Firms	Associations	Local	Foreign	Joint	Chinese	Other	Selangor	Rest
Cooperation	21	53	23	16	27	22	25	21	25
Do not have cooperation	79	47	77	84	73	78	75	79	75

The researchers were rather surprised at the low percentage of cooperation among associations, but the apparent result may be due to conscious false under-reporting. Many firms, however, reported privately that communal associations were not very effective, and poorer Penang firm managers noted that fees for the large manufacturing associations were too high—thus they did not attempt to join.

As interesting were the types of firms with whom they reportedly cooperated. Only 10% of the firms in the national sample stated that they cooperated with companies in the same field, and no foreign firm so stated. The latter statement is particularly suspect, as in Penang the greatest cooperation in the area was among foreign electronics firms over problems with labor and government-provided infrastructure. Also notable is the fact that only one percent of the Chinese firms were prepared to state that they cooperated with associations. It is my view that this type of interaction was severely under-reported, perhaps because interviewees feared being charged with illegal collusion.

When we attempted to pursue the issue by asking if firms used nongovernmental groups for assistance when they had an interest in a particular government activity, a somewhat different picture appeared. Approximately two-fifths of our respondents in the national sample answered affirmatively to the question, "More particularly when your company (org.) has an interest in a specific government activity, do you contact any nongovernmental group for assistance?" Percentages ranged from 37% to 46%, except for Chinese firms, of which only 32% were willing to answer affirmatively.

What emerges from this questioning of heads of firms is high awareness of government programs, infrequent contact with officials on the input side of government but considerable contact with administrators, low reported cooperation with other firms in influencing government but a rather high percentage prepared to admit to the use of private go-betweens in dealing with specific government problems. We can conjecture that considerably more cooperation with other companies and contact with politicians takes place than was admitted to the interviewers.

RESULTS OF INFORMATION AND CONTACTS

Two areas of results from information and contacts were investigated: the obtaining of government contracts and the question of self-efficacy. We wished to discover whether a particular type of organization was better informed, more aware and more capable of gaining the rewards of data and contacts than other types. First, approximately 27% of all firms directly or indirectly participate in federal government projects (see table 5), with a somewhat lower percentage involved in state projects (approximately 22%).

TABLE 5
PARTICIPATION IN FEDERAL GOVERNMENT PROJECTS
(In percentages)

	Total firms	Local	Foreign	Joint	Chinese	Other	Selangor	Rest
Direct current participation	21	19	16	31	16	18	25	12
Indirect—reap benefits	6	6	13	2	4	9	4	7

It is significant that firms owned by local Chinese and firms based in outlying areas have been less fortunate than others in securing government contracts, and that joint venture firms are more successful. In part, this is a result of official efforts to aid Malay firms and government participation in joint venture projects with foreign firms. The lower Chinese participation is also partially due to the fact that a significantly lower percentage of Chinese firms are aware of government projects (only 66% as against 87% for firms owned by other nationalities). As well, foreign firms have been reluctant to establish factories or develop contacts in outlying areas lacking adequate economic infrastructure to sustain profitable activities.

Finally, there is the question of self-efficacy, the perception by the firm management of its company's ability to change government policies. The question asked the two hundred forty-five firms and associations was, "How effective do you believe that your company (org.) has been in gaining desired changes in government policies?

Very effective?
Quite effective?
Somewhat ineffective?
Ineffective?
Never tried?"

The majority reported their firms to be somewhat ineffective, to be ineffective, or as never having tried to influence government. The most effective in their own view were joint venture firms and the associations, along with respondents in some outlying states who apparently felt effective in dealing with local authorities (see table 6).

TABLE 6
SELF-PERCEIVED EFFECTIVENESS
(In percentages)

	Total firms	Association	Local	Foreign	Joint	Chinese	Other	Selangor	Rest
Very effective	6	12	4	6	11	4	9	4	8
Quite effective	25	59	24	23	37	22	37	24	30
Somewhat effective	34	12	39	19	23	42	14	25	40
Ineffective	21	18	20	29	16	22	18	25	16
Never tried	15	0	13	23	13	10	22	22	6

This was a rather remarkable admission of frustration on the part of a sample of the largest firms in Malaysia (similar results were gained from small firms in Penang). Among all groups of firms no types reported a majority feeling effective and in most cases the percentage was only about 30 to 40%.

One might ask whether there is a particular pattern of awareness, contact, and effectiveness among the groups concerned. An effort was made to see whether there was an interrelationship among these three variables and then to assess the composition of the groups concerned. A definite pattern did emerge.

1. Those with the highest contacts with political leaders tended to be better informed, cooperated with other firms to a greater extent, and had higher self perceptions of success. This was particularly true regarding those who had more frequent contacts with ministers, MPs, and senators. A declining pattern was maintained across respondents categorized as having high, medium, and low contacts.

2. Those who were able to participate directly or indirectly in federal government projects were more likely to be better informed and to cooperate with others, but there was no statistically significant difference between high and low respondents regarding contacts and perceptions of influence except that those with medium contacts tended to be less successful.

3. Those firms using nongovernmental groups for assistance were more likely to be informed and to work with others, but there were not important differences in the other categories.

4. Those with the highest perceptions of influence tended to be better informed, to have more frequent contacts with government, and to cooperate more with others.

REASONS FOR MEANS OF INFLUENCE

We have noted the primary emphasis given to influencing the output as against the input elements of government in the Malaysian case. Our next task is to analyze the reasons for this pattern of influence. Fragmentary evidence from other Afro-Asian states tends to substantiate the style of interaction. Furthermore, we should comment that not all interest groups tend to act as does business in Malaysia, or elsewhere in Afro-Asia. Mass organizations, "official" groups such as civil servants and elements of political parties, as well as what have been called "whole life" interest groups (religious, racial, tribal, and communally oriented segments of society) may attempt to put pressure on the input functions of government, both within and without the system.[4] We are concentrating in this paper, however, on private interest groups, and most particularly upon economic organizations; and in this narrower framework four major explanatory factors related to primary influence on the output functions appear to be the most important: 1) attitudes toward interest group activity; 2) the precarious position of the private economic sector; 3) ownership of firms; and 4) other means of access to government. While all these elements are relevant in Malaysia, they have general validity for the rest of Afro-Asia, and are even more important in some other countries.

1. *Attitudes.* M. Esman has strongly asserted that Malaysia's civil service finds interference by politicians and interest groups less than attractive.[5] As in so many former colonies, the administrator in the past was the individual who both made the regulations and saw that they were followed. Rising business interests and political parties were suspect.

> The danger civil servants see for Malaysia is that the petty and corrupt politics of aggressive individual and small-group interests may destroy both legitimate politics and administration. . . . Malaysia's civil servants distrust the political process of pressure, influence, and expedient bargaining, and they distrust as well the political role.[6]

In the case of Malaysia, large-scale manufacturing and commercial interests are relatively new (except for mines, plantations, and agency houses) and the economic and political role of large firms is still evolving.[7]

Malaysian firms themselves believe that it is "improper" for the private sector to attempt to influence the formulation of government policies. In interviews with Malaysian firm owners and managers, a number of respondents volunteered that they did not believe that firms should behave in this way. Not one respondent stated that he would attempt to engage in any pressure group activities to change the New Economic Policy, although a sizable minority were dissatisfied with some elements of the NEP.[8] At the same time, firms stated their willingness to attempt to influence laws and regulations that would affect their firms and 8% of the respondents (mostly local Chinese) commented that they did not intend fully implementing the NEP, anyway.

In sum, attitudes of both civil servants and firms support a belief in the rightness of operating in an environment that generally precludes public efforts by private interest groups to influence government policies, but firms do attempt to get civil servants to interpret laws and regulations in their favor.

2. *Role of the private sector.* While the private sector is less vulnerable to government interference or seizure in Malaysia than in most Afro-Asian states, many intellectuals and politicians hold private enterprise in suspicion. The restrictive role of such suspicions is far more obvious in socialist countries, where the private sector is often considered as an unwelcome and sometimes temporary phenomenon, than in capitalist states. While ostensibly Malaysia is strongly in favor of the private sector, efforts to increase Malay ownership of the modern sector through the NEP and politically-oriented attacks on working conditions in factories have made non-Malay owned firms wary.[9] These attacks have come from the traditional right and the small socialist left, both of which have harassed industrial firms. Such criticism leads to caution against acting in ways which might engender public outcries against "improper" interference in politics.

3. *Ownership.* Wariness is understandable in light of the racial and national composition of major firms in Malaysia. The modern sector of the economy is dominated by two major groups. The largest with respect to its share in investments is the foreign investor. A combination of British, Japanese, American, Hong Kong, Singaporean, and other foreign managers' and owners' activities controls approximately two-thirds of the modern economic sector of Malaysia. Even though these firms tend to pay higher wages and make efforts to meet the Malay employment quota standards of the NEP,[10] they are frequently attacked by politicians and intellectuals. Given the now fashionable nature of criticism of multinationals in the third world, foreign companies are particularly careful not to appear to be interfering in Malaysia's political process. They do make vigorous efforts to get favorable treatment under the laws and often make representations to state and federal government over problems with infrastructure, visas, education for expatriate children, etc. Also, birthdays of national leaders bring large advertisements of congratulations and annual reports at times include praise of the country's political elite.

The other major group is the local Chinese, who are active at all levels of the economy, particularly in tin production, construction, and commercial enterprises from small family-based firms to large financial institutions. In spite of the statistically smaller role of the Chinese in the modern sector, as compared with foreigners (less than 30%), the majority of the

Malay community perceives them as dominating the local economy. In part this is because smaller Chinese firms are in more immediate contact with the poorer Malays, engaged as they are in small commercial activities such as stores, rice mills, theaters, restaurants, and so on. In the initial years of independence there was general agreement that the Malays would control the political and administrative life of the country while the Chinese would dominate the commercial sector. Since the racially-oriented riots of May 1969, the Malaysian political elite has sought to bring the Malays into the modern sector through government efforts. The stated goal is to have the Chinese and Indians own 40%, foreigners 30%, and Malays 30% of the modern enterprises. While no group is supposed to have total investments decline (because of expected economic growth), the largest increase is to be among the Malay, who now own approximately 2%. The combination of Malay perceptions of Chinese dominance and government programs to expand Malay participation in the economy makes the Chinese economic community careful about public political activity.

A further reason for caution among the Chinese has been a tendency for Chinese business to consider that political activities are not desirable. For many years the Chinese did not have full rights of citizenship and some Chinese felt themselves only temporary residents. Neither of these factors is now particularly relevant, but they have colored the attitudes of older Chinese merchants. This is especially true of the more traditional entrepreneurs who are not fully familiar with the new political-bureaucratic system.

It should be emphasized that neither the foreign nor the Chinese economic community is as vulnerable to attack as in most other South or Southeast Asian states. Malaysia remains eager to encourage foreign investment and offers a variety of incentives for industries considered desirable by the government. Also, the size of the Chinese population (approximately 37%) and efforts to establish a multi-national political system make them considerably more secure than most of their neighboring counterparts. These factors do not, however, make them invulnerable to attack from politicians across the political spectrum.

4. *Access.* We have noted a hesitancy to employ Western-style public interest group activities. In part this is due to opportunities to develop more private means of influence including personal contacts, putting prominent Malaysians on boards of directors, financial support, etc. These allow the knowledgeable firm representative to obtain government support through unobtrusive means. It should be emphasized that this pattern is far less important than in other Southeast Asian states such as Thailand, the Philippines, and Indonesia, where in previous years private financial "arrangements" between the public and private sectors were flagrant. In Thailand,

prior to the 1973 government change, it was normal practice for Chinese firms to put civil and military officials on their boards for the purposes of both protection and access. In Malaysia non-public contacts between the public and private sectors remain an important means of getting across the firm's point of view, but less frequently and with considerably less corruption than has been present in other Southeast Asian states. To the degree that such access is available, however, the "normal" means of pressure group activity is not necessary.

In sum, then, most large Malaysian firms find the American style of interest group politics dangerous, unattractive, or unnecessary. Their international or racial composition puts them in too vulnerable a position to participate publicly in influencing major government programs, even though government may have a significant impact on their business activities. It is only when the very existence of the firm is threatened that it moves into the public arena, and examples of such activities are rare. Moreover, the better managed firms have found public efforts to influence the input functions of government less vitally necessary than might be expected. The firm maintains regular means of obtaining knowledge of government policies and regulations, is in frequent contact with elements of the civil service, and has often found other, less public, means of obtaining redress of grievances.

The aforementioned pattern of interest group policies should not be taken to mean that firms are completely pleased with present arrangements. On the whole, however, they have been able to operate successfully in Malaysia with acceptable profits and less danger of expropriation than in most other South or Southeast Asian states. It should also be noted that the major complaints voiced by firms have been either incapable of redress through public action or not of a nature necessitating pressure on the administration. As an example, the major objection to the Malay quota system for employment cannot be openly attacked because of a constitutional prohibition against raising racial issues. On the other hand, the almost universal complaint against government red tape cannot easily be solved through parliamentary action, if it can be ameliorated at all.[11]

Finally, it is doubtful that this pattern of influence will change radically in the future. Firms feel increasingly vulnerable to political attack and the government is actively attempting to increase its own involvement in industry. Politicians now find baiting foreign and Chinese owned firms to be politically rewarding, and even greater caution is proving necessary now than previously. Nationalism is growing in Malaysia to add to difficulties, and government efforts to increase Malay ownership in the modern sector through buying into large companies raises the specter of future expropriation. All of this limits pressure on the input functions of government and demands greater reliance on employing influence on the output functions.

NOTES

1. Of firms interviewed the following samples were obtained:
A. Local 152, foreign 31, joint ownership 62;
B. Selangor 121, Northern states 59, Negri Sembilan and Malacca 19, Jahore 27, East Coast 19;
C. Chinese ownership or associations 158, other 87;
D. Primary Products 42, Western Trading 20, Asian Trading 43, Food Manufacturing 22, Engineering 22, Other Manufacturers 36, Services 19, Finance 24.

2. The NEP is a recent Malaysian government program which seeks to eradicate poverty and raise the economic and social standards of the Malay. See F. R. von der Mehden, "Communalism, Industrial Policy and Income Distribution in Malaysia," *Asian Survey* **15**, No. 3 (March, 1975): 250-261.

3. The small percentage of Selangor firms is due to the large number of foreign firms based there.

4. Studies in other developing countries have shown the importance of mass organizations. See, for example, J. Silverstein, "Burmese and Malaysian Student Politics," *Journal of Southeast Asian Studies* **1**, No. 1 (March, 1970): 3-22; J. R. Gusfield, "Political Community and Group Interests in Modern India," *Pacific Affairs* **38**, No. 2 (Summer, 1965): 123-141; T. Manirurwanam, "Group Interests in Pakistan Politics, 1947-58," *Pacific Affairs* **39**, Nos. 1 and 2 (Spring-Summer, 1966): 83-98.

5. M. Esman, *Administration and Development in Malaysia* (Ithaca: Cornell University Press, 1972), pp. 124-128.

6. Ibid. pp. 125-126.

7. In 1938 there were only 77 manufacturing concerns in the Federated Malay States employing more than ten workers, and in the Unfederated Malay States about 300 of all sizes and kinds, mostly producing for the local market. Kate Mitchell, *Industrialization of the Western Pacific* (New York: IPR, 1942), pp. 184-187. This grew to Secondary Industry firms totalling 139,619 employees in 1947 and 203,516 in 1957. The majority of firms, however, still employed less than 10 workers in 1957. E. L. Wheelwright, "Industrialization in Malaya," in *The Political Economy of Independent Malaya,* ed. T. H. Silcock (Berkeley, Calif.: University of California Press, 1963).

8. In part this reluctance is due to constitutional restrictions prohibiting attacks on basic assumptions upon which the Malaysian state is now founded.

9. See von der Mehden, "Communalism, Industrial Policy and Income Distribution in Malaysia."

10. The government has attempted to establish a policy of having firms reflect the national composition of the population at all levels. In practice this has meant efforts to install 40% quotas for Malays at least below the management level. Ibid.

11. Interestingly enough, spokesmen in company headquarters abroad are far more favorably impressed with the ease of doing business in Malaysia than are local managers. In part, this is due to more difficult problems in other countries and the distance from the nitty-gritty difficulties met by managers in the field.

II

DOMESTIC ISSUES

GROWTH AND EQUITY IN DEVELOPING ECONOMIES

by Ronald Soligo

INTRODUCTION

Economists have generally relegated a concern for the personal distribution of income and wealth to a quite separate and isolated place within the discipline. With some exceptions, focus has been placed on questions of resource allocation and efficiency, areas in which it was felt that relatively "value free" statements could be made. Studies of the personal distribution of income have been made, but the distribution of income is usually presented as an outcome of the economic system, with little said about the desirability of one distribution over another, though perhaps with the tacit understanding that a more equitable distribution was "better" than a less equitable one on the basis of humanitarian concerns. Since changes in income distribution are generally perceived as situations in which some people are made better off and others worse off, however, it has always been difficult to lend any "scientific" rigor to a ranking of distributions. One had to admit that it is operationally impossible to measure in any meaningful way the gains and losses actually experienced by different people, and thus be able to determine whether the sum of total happiness had been increased or decreased by the redistribution.

To the extent that the distribution of income has been seen to have a causal role in determining economic variables, as distinct from being determined by them, that role lay in the interrelationship between the distribution of income on the one hand and the savings rate on the other. The savings rate in turn was a primary determinant of the growth rate of output. This view of economic growth has its origins in the work of the classical economists who argued that it was the entrepreneurial class, whose income was derived from profits, that did most of the saving and investing in an economy. Laborers were too poor to have any income left over for saving after meeting the needs of subsistence. The rentier class indulged in ostentatious living and also saved little. The key to rapid expansion of

Mr. Soligo is Professor of Economics and Director of the Program of Development Studies at Rice University.

productive capacity, output, and employment was to maximize the share of total income that accrued to the entrepreneurial class. Greater distributional equity, which would increase the incomes of the poor at the expense of this class, would reduce savings and hence the growth of output. There was, then, a trade-off. Greater inequity today would be rewarded by greater output tomorrow; greater equity today would be purchased at the cost of a smaller national income tomorrow. Classical economists never considered the possibility of a trade-off between output and employment. For them, maximum output was consistent with, and indeed, equivalent to a situation of maximum employment.

This model of economic growth is a very simplified one, which leaves out many other important variables determining the interrelationships among output, employment, and distributional equity. In particular, it focuses only on the interrelationship between income distribution and savings and between savings and the growth rate of output. But the growth rate of output is also determined by the incremental capital output ratio (the amount of investment required to expand by one dollar) and the rate of technological change. Also, since a large part of the capital goods needed for growth must be imported from the more advanced countries that have already developed the capacity to produce these goods, the growth rate of output will be influenced by the ability to export and the extent to which foreign exchange resources are used to finance imports of investment goods rather than consumer goods.

Similarly, the rate of growth and the skill structure of employment are not simple functions of the rate of growth of output, but depend on the composition of that growth, the type of bias in new technologies being introduced, and the extent to which labor can be substituted for capital in each sector of the economy. Some industries are more labor-intensive than others; some use relatively more skilled labor, others more unskilled labor. Finally, some industries have access to labor-saving technology; in other cases, new technology may have a more capital-saving basis.

The classical model did not explore the possibility that different growth strategies, defined in accordance with those sectors and industries which grew the most quickly, might have different incremental capital output ratios, different levels and biases of technological change, different effects on employment, different levels of exports, and different levels of imports of consumption goods. Nor did they explore the interrelationship between the distribution of income and the pattern of growth that was likely to emerge.

It is quite clear, however, that the pattern of growth will reflect the distribution of income. The pattern of private investment and production will be responsive to the structure of effective demand. If the income distribution is highly skewed in favor of the rich, then resources will be devoted to such items as automobile production, U. S. franchised food establishments, and other industries producing goods and services needed to sustain the Western-oriented life styles of the high income groups. Exports will be used to finance luxury consumer goods and investment goods needed to produce these consumption goods and services domestically. Despite the fact that much of this production might seem frivolous in comparison to the needs of the majority of the people for a decent diet, shelter, clothing, sanitation, and medical care, the fact is that the poor do not have the income to make their needs felt in the marketplace.

While public investment need not respond to market forces and could be directed toward building the capacity to produce goods and services consumed by low income groups, in general this does not happen. In the first place, the distribution of political power generally reflects the distribution of income. Hence public expenditures often reflect the need for public services by the higher income groups. In addition, however, the pattern of development that is based on the consumption patterns of the higher income groups, a pattern which emphasizes urban development and large-scale industrialization, requires a substantial investment in relatively large capital-intensive projects such as electric power generation and modern transport facilities. In most cases, only the government has access to the quantity of capital necessary to finance these investments or is willing to take on the risks of such projects where the initial investment can be recovered only in a relatively long period of time. After meeting these needs, the government typically has few resources available for other uses.

The argument for neglecting the effects of the changes in the structure of output on the growth of output and employment and on income distribution is that, whatever the structure, benefits will filter down to provide more employment and income to the vast majority of the people. But this view neglects the fact that the extent to which benefits filter down is a function of the pattern of growth. The poor will benefit more when expansion occurs in industries utilizing relatively large amounts of unskilled labor rather than in industries employing relatively small amounts. Further, output will grow at a faster rate when expansion occurs predominantly in industries using relatively little capital and imported inputs. Thus different development strategies can have different effects on employment, equity, and growth of output. An important issue is the extent to which the interrelationship among these variables counteracts or eliminates the classical trade-off between growth and equity.

Aside from the theoretical complications involving the interrelationships among equity, employment, and output, there is the empirical experience of some twenty-five years of concerted development effort by the developing economies and the aid-giving nations. The results of this experience are not encouraging. Large groups in most developing countries have been untouched by the massive efforts undertaken there. Unemployment and income inequalities have been increasing in many countries, producing political and social pressures that are on a scale unprecedented in world economic development. Therefore, the search for a better understanding of the determinants of employment, output, and distribution has an immediacy independent of scholarly interest. In particular, it is important to know to what extent these goals must be traded off with one another and whether there are alternative policies and strategies that would eliminate or reduce the trade-offs.

THE TRADE-OFF BETWEEN GROWTH AND EQUITY

Before looking at the effect of economic structure on growth and equity, one should consider a more conventional neoclassical argument that focuses on the short-run as distinct from a long-run situation.

One crucial assumption implicit in the classical theory is that all resources are being employed efficiently. It is this assumption which creates the trade-off between equity and output; more income for the poor must be accompanied by less for the rich—hence, less savings and less output growth. As Wayne Thirsk argues in this volume, however, most developing economies are characterized by serious inefficiencies in resource use so that it is, in principle, possible to have both greater equity and more output if those inefficiencies can be reduced. The qualification is important since most of the inefficiencies result from price distortions that benefit the privileged groups—the very groups which, in large measure, control economic policy in these countries. Also, the relaxation of the equity-output trade-off will only be temporary. Once resource use becomes efficient, we will return to the long-run world where the trade-off of the classical theory will hold.

While Thirsk illustrates his argument in the context of the agricultural sector, it applies equally to policies affecting the industrial sector. Consistently one finds that tax, trade, foreign exchange, and commercial policies are constructed so as to subsidize and encourage the use of capital at the expense of the overabundant factor of production, labor. As a result, scarce savings are not efficiently used to maximize the increase in output; and actual output increases are less than they could be, given those resources. The choice of capital-intensive modes of production also leads to relatively less employment generation, given the increase in output, and the new employment often favors the scarce workers with technical skills rather than those in most need, who have few skills.

It should be pointed out that even in a world of unfettered competition the use of labor in developing economies would be discouraged. Even though unskilled labor is greatly underemployed and in some cases unemployed so that, from a social point of view, it has zero cost (its employment would not decrease output in any other part of the economy), individuals will not work and forgo leisure unless they are paid a positive wage. Since employers must pay this positive wage they will base their hiring decisions on it rather than on the true social cost of zero. Hence they will hire fewer workers than is socially efficient. Also, although labor is abundant, it is truly unskilled labor, lacking even rudimentary experience with an industrial system. Finally, since labor-intensive production processes obviously require a relatively larger supervisory and managerial staff than more capital-intensive modes, the latter are often favored because of the extreme shortage of supervisory personnel.

In addition to these fundamental problems in the functioning of the labor market, there are even more serious difficulties with capital markets, which are rudimentary and fragmented. The undeveloped state of capital markets means that savings cannot be allocated to their most efficient uses. The linkages between savers and investors are so weak that for the most part investors are forced to finance their expenditures from their own savings, and savers are required either to find profitable investment opportunities on their own or to accept rates of interest which are usually less than the rate of inflation. In this type of economy the pattern of investment tends to reflect the interests of the individuals who have investable resources rather than the uses which are most profitable from a social point of view.

Such structural defects in the labor and capital markets are responsive to government policy. Even if policy choices are wisely made, however, improvements in these markets will require a great deal of time. Unfortunately, governments (and aid-giving agencies) do not give sufficient attention to long-run solutions. The immediate economic, political, and social pressures invariably preoccupy the limited resources of time, thought, energy, and money available to policy makers. As a result, very little has been done in the past to rectify the more fundamental problems of the factor markets. Even if attention is given to these problems now, no immediate and large increase in efficiency can be expected in the short run.

Results can be achieved more readily in the short run by removing the distortions in markets and prices that are the result of activist government policy. Resisting pressures to increase urban minimum wage rates will encourage greater employment, equity, and output. The same can be said for the removal of import controls and foreign exchange policies that subsidize the use of capital. While it is clear, however, that, other things being equal, the removal of specific restrictions to the functioning of the market will lead to more employment and output, it is less clear that doing so will increase the degree of distributional equity.

The uncertainty with respect to the effect on equity arises from several sources. First, one must distinguish between changes in the level of income and changes in the distribution of income. Removal of market restrictions may lead to an increase in total income and to an increase in the income of the poor. Yet it may, in addition, increase the income of the wealthy, and that increase may exceed the increase accruing to the poor. In principle, a situation in which everyone has a higher income even though the distribution of that income is more unequal should be viewed as an improvement. An individual's sense of well-being, however, is often determined by the level of his income *relative* to the incomes of other individuals with whom he has some contact. In other words, distribution *per se* may be an important determinant of whether or not one feels better off. In political terms, the distribution of gains from growth may be even more important than the amount of growth.[1]

A second factor is that there are very few situations in which a change in policy would make everyone better off. Typically, changes in policy will make some people worse off. For example, while it is clear that the removal or reduction of urban minimum wages would help many low income persons by encouraging employers to use more labor, and hence provide more employment, those who initially benefited from the minimum wage would suffer a reduction in income. An overall index of equality may show an increase, but there may be specific individuals who are in, say, the bottom half of the income distribution who would be hurt.

Thirdly, what might be appropriate for the current period may not hold for the longer run. For example, removal of restraints on market behavior could lead to a situation in which equity is immediately improved, but in which there will be even greater inequalities in the future. This situation would occur if the policy change increased the incomes of all groups and if the high income groups either saved a significantly larger portion of their income or received a significantly higher rate of return on their savings than the lower income groups. In the long run the distribution of wealth, and hence the distribution of income from that wealth, will become increasingly unequal. In this example there is no trade-off between output and equity in the short run, but in the longer run a trade-off exists because of the growing disparities in the ownership of wealth. Other examples of this nature are discussed in the next section.

The efficacy of an employment and income distribution policy that focuses on improving the functioning of markets ultimately rests on how easily market distortions can be eliminated and on the response of the economic system to changes in various prices. Some problems associated with improving the operation of markets have been discussed above. They include problems of creating market institutions, and the political problems of disturbing the status quo. The response of decision makers to price changes depends largely on the degree of substitutability of various factors of production in the production process and of various goods and services in the consumption patterns of households. The degree of this substitutability is controversial and eventually must be settled empirically. To some extent, however, the degree to which one can rely on responses to relative price changes is a political as well as a technical problem. For example, even if firms could substitute labor for capital in large enough quantities to make a significant difference in employment, the extent to which prices of labor and capital might have to change in order to induce firms to undertake this substitution might not be politically feasible. Similar conclusions hold on the consumption side where households are very inflexible in their consumption patterns.

ECONOMIC STRUCTURE, OUTPUT, AND EMPLOYMENT

As seen in the previous section, the conclusion that greater reliance on well-functioning markets will lead to more output, employment, and perhaps equity, needs to be qualified in light of the degree of factor substitutability in production processes. In a world in which there is underutilized labor and limited factor substitutability, and in which different industries use factor inputs in different proportions, the level and rate of growth of output and employment will be a function of the composition of production. Hence the level of employment could be increased in both the short and long run by altering the product mix.

To see this we need a model which interconnects income (or wealth) distribution, consumption patterns, and relative factor intensities. James Land and I have constructed such a model, in which we show that under certain assumptions, other things being equal, it is possible to have more output and employment if income and wealth are more equitably distributed.[2] Our model is based on three assumptions: 1) that low income families tend to consume goods and services which on the average are more labor-intensive (i.e., use more labor and less capital per unit of output) than high income families; 2) that there is limited factor substitutability in the production of goods and services (this assumption permits some range of choices involving different input combinations, but asserts that there are some binding limits on the degree to which labor can replace capital in various production processes); 3) that the marginal propensity to save (the proportion of changes in disposable income that is saved) is the same for all income classes.

The logic of the model can be seen as follows. If we consider two income groups, the rich and the poor; two factors of production, homogeneous labor and capital; two goods, S (simple) goods which are labor-intensive and C goods which are capital-intensive; then, if each income class consumes the same proportion of an increment in income and the rich spend a higher proportion of their income on C goods than do the poor, a transfer of one dollar from rich to poor will increase the level of employment. In addition, the total level of output produced with the given amount of capital increases because the new output mix of C and S goods uses less capital than the previous mix.[3]

In this model there is no trade-off between equity and growth, so long as the marginal propensity to save is the same for the two income classes. Indeed, the pattern of growth that is characterized by a greater degree of equity will permit a higher rate of growth of output and employment, since each increment in output requires a smaller investment in capital.

To the extent that the marginal savings propensity of the rich, following the classical assumption, is greater than that of the poor, the rate of growth in employment and output following redistribution will be smaller than where marginal savings propensities were the same. When savings propensities differ by a relatively large amount, when the difference in the capital intensity of C and S goods is relatively small, or when the relative proportion in which the two income classes consume the two goods is similar, a case develops in which the negative effect on growth rates arising from the reduction in savings more than offsets the positive effect of a reduction in the overall capital intensity of the product mix. These two effects have been labeled the savings effect and the demand-compositional effect.

The relative importance of the two effects must be settled empirically. It is interesting to note, however, that the *a priori* judgments by economists differ considerably. A group of economists, in a report on employment and income distribution in Colombia prepared for the International Labour Organization, placed the major emphasis on the demand-compositional effect, while a model constructed by economists at the World Bank ignores this effect entirely and considers only the savings effect.[4] Empirical work that has been completed to date is discussed below.

In the context of the theoretical model, the transfer of income could be achieved by levying a tax on the rich and transferring the revenue to the poor, or by redistributing the ownership of wealth from the rich to the poor. In practice, of course, it may not be possible or practical to redistribute existing wealth. Rather, policies can be adopted which lead to a different distribution of increments to national wealth. These policies can range from making education and skill acquisition (human capital) more accessible to low income groups, to facilitating changes in the capital market that allow the poor to obtain higher returns on their savings.

Policies that focus on removing price distortions in order to encourage the substitution of labor for capital in production will, of course, increase output and employment. But the extent to which these variables will increase is a function of the possibilities for substitution within each industry. On the other hand, policies that focus on increasing the proportion of wealth held by the poor can lead to increased output and employment even if substitution within each industry is limited, since reliance is placed on shifts in the pattern of consumption and production towards more labor using industries. Furthermore, to the extent that equity is a specific policy objective, that objective is best achieved by the latter type of policy, which focuses directly on the distribution of wealth, rather than the former, which has a more indirect effect on equity.

To some extent policies designed to influence the distribution of wealth will also serve to stimulate input substitution within firms. For example, import licensing procedures that allocate foreign exchange to large-scale industrialists for the importation of foreign-made machinery clearly discriminate against the small-scale entrepreneur in making it more difficult for him to obtain capital goods. Removal of licensing would permit small-scale firms to expand more rapidly and put more capital in the hands of people who are relatively poor. At the same time large-scale firms will be induced to economize on capital inputs when these are no longer subsidized, and will seek ways of utilizing labor where they might previously have used machinery. Another example is discussed by Huddle and Ho in their paper in this volume. They point out the problems faced by small-scale firms in obtaining credit in a system in which banks, because of restrictions on the interest rates they can charge for loans, necessarily prefer to allocate credit to large enterprises, which pose a smaller risk. Removal of interest rate ceilings would both permit small-scale firms to invest more (by financing the acquisition of new capital goods by bank loans) and induce large firms to use less capital, and more labor, in their production activities.

If policy making and implementation were costless, one obviously would recommend that governments undertake both kinds of policies. Unfortunately, policy development and administration require highly skilled resources. Furthermore, many policy moves will meet with some political opposition, which either limits the application of that policy or requires resources to overcome it. In either case, governments must make choices as to where they will focus their attention. Many will argue, with some justification, that emphasis on market function without a specific focus on income distribution has never been given a fair test. Nonetheless, political pressures in developing countries seem to be pushing policy initiatives towards addressing the equity issue immediately.

EMPIRICAL WORK

While the theoretical model outlined in the previous section shows that greater distributional equity could be consistent with higher growth rates of output and employment, this conclusion rests on several assumptions. These include the assumptions that low income groups tend to consume more labor-intensive goods and services than higher income groups and that the marginal savings propensities of the higher income groups are not significantly higher than those of the lower income groups.

A great deal of research has been completed on comparing the relative labor intensity of consumption patterns of various income classes;[5] relatively little has been done on measuring differential savings propensities. Conclusions to date tend to support the Land-Soligo hypothesis, that the low income groups tend to consume relatively more of labor-intensive goods and services, although the support is not unequivocal.

The most significant change in expenditure patterns as one moves from low income to high income families is in the proportion of income spent on food. This ratio declines from roughly 50% to 20% for most of the LDCs. If one looks at expenditures from changes in income (marginal expenditure coefficients) the decline is even greater. In some cases the poor will spend as much as 80% of increments to income on food while the richest groups have already achieved an excellent diet and will spend very little extra on food with increases in income.

The importance of the different propensities to consume food lies in the fact that the production of food is much more labor-intensive (requires more labor per unit of output) than many other activities. Hence, when a more egalitarian growth strategy is adopted, the composition of consumption and output shifts in favor of the agricultural sector, producing significant effects on the level of employment of unskilled labor and thus reinforcing the overall equity of the distribution of income.

An unexpected result, however, is that the amount of capital required per unit of agricultural output is not much lower than in other sectors of the economy, so that the shift in output mix does not reduce the aggregate capital-output ratio as much as anticipated. Thus although redistribution has a very large impact on employment, it has a much more modest effect on the growth rate of output.

The apparent paradox of a sector using both more capital and labor than other sectors arises because the overall efficiency of agriculture is extremely low relative to the efficiency of the others.

Improving agricultural efficiency thus becomes a key prerequisite to an income-distribution-oriented growth strategy. New agricultural technologies, such as new high yielding varieties which are more resistant to disease and more responsive to applications of fertilizer and water, are particularly important since they are essentially capital and land saving in nature. With these technologies redistribution would have a much greater impact on both employment and output growth than under traditional technologies.

The proportion of income spent on non-agricultural goods and services also differs among income groups, and changes in the distribution of income will change the relative importance of these in total output. These changes in the non-agricultural output mix, however, tend to have much less effect on total employment or the aggregate capital-output ratio than the shift in output composition towards more agricultural output relative to non-agricultural output.[6]

While many economists have attempted to measure the impact of redistribution on growth via its effect on the aggregate savings rate (the savings effect), their methodology suffers from serious conceptual problems and hence their conclusions must be discounted.

The methodology employed is to take cross section data on family income and expenditure from a household budget survey and to fit a statistical relationship between family income and savings. This relationship is used to estimate the effect of different income distributions on personal savings. It assumes that these data do, in fact, measure the marginal savings propensities of various income classes.

There is a vast literature dealing with the methodological and theoretical problems of measuring savings behavior.[7] Suffice it to say here that, in general, the use of cross section data will tend to overstate the inter-income differences in savings behavior. At this point, the issue of whether there is a negative savings effect of sufficient magnitude to counteract the positive effects on growth of the reduced capital-output ratio (which results from a shift in the composition of output toward the goods and services consumed by the poor) must remain open until further empirical work has been done.

In addition to the usual problems of measuring marginal savings propensities, there is another important issue in the context of the less developed economies. We have already referred above to the fact that capital markets in less developed countries are undeveloped and fragmented so that savers have few profitable opportunities to employ their savings. In most countries the available opportunities consist of holding one's savings in cash or in bank accounts that typically pay a very low nominal rate of interest controlled by law, or investing the funds in some form of real capital (land, human capital, or plant and equipment). Holding cash or bank deposits generally yields a significantly negative rate of return, since the rate of price inflation is very much higher than the nominal interest rates paid on these assets. On the other hand, not all savers have either the interest or the expertise necessary to invest in real (as distinct from financial) assets. The result is that the return to savings and wealth accumulation, and hence the incentive to save, is reduced. Since the lack of profitable savings opportunities affects the lower income groups more than the higher income groups, the lack of a developed and well-functioning capital market will bias savings decisions in a way that reduces the propensity to save by the poor relative to that of the rich. The bias is magnified by a standard convention followed by economists when measuring consumption and savings, which counts the acquisition of consumer durables such as sewing machines, radios, furniture, bicycles, etc. (except houses), as consumption rather than investment. Yet all of these are durable goods that will produce consumption services over a period of several years. That is, these goods, like any investment good, will serve the household over a long period of time and not solely in the year in which the expenditure is made. The bias is not critical in a developed economy such as the United States where the service income produced by consumer durables is typically small relative to total family income. (An exception is the retired couple whose money income is very small but whose real income is quite satisfactory because of the service income produced by the house, car, and other durables purchased in earlier years.) For less developed countries, the bias is important because the service income is large relative to money income and because the acquisition of such consumer durables is usually the most productive use, given the state of capital markets, for the savings of lower income families. Counting the acquisition of consumer durables as savings (and investment) and increasing the range of assets as well as the real rates of return available to low income groups will increase the measured and real savings of low income groups. These factors further reinforce the conclusion that at this point there is no reason to believe that a negative savings effect is likely to be significant.

SUMMARY

This paper has reviewed the issues regarding the interrelationship between distributional equity and the growth rate of output and employment in developing economies. This issue is one which has been neglected until very recently. Classical economists viewed the relationship in terms of a trade-off. Greater equity reduced the savings rate and hence the growth of output and employment.

Neoclassical economists, with their emphasis on efficient resource allocation, have shown that in the short run at least there need not be a trade-off. Most developing economies have many market distortions, which lead to serious misallocation of resources. By correcting these distortions output *and* employment could be increased. Whether this would always lead to a higher degree of distributional equity as measured by some inequality index is not always certain, but it is clear that the lower income groups as a whole would benefit by having higher real incomes.

More recent models of development have attempted to incorporate income distribution, output, and employment determination more formally. Given certain assumptions about the relative factor intensity of consumption patterns and marginal savings propensities of different income classes, we show that, in contrast to the classical model, greater equity could be consistent with higher growth rates of output and employment. The empirical evidence to date is not definitive but tends to give encouraging support to the assumptions made in the model.

The issues addressed in this paper are of importance to the theoretical economist who is interested in knowing more about the role that income distribution plays in the determination of other economic variables and, conversely, the variables that in turn determine the distribution of income. The issues also have an important real world immediacy. The problems of poverty and unemployment faced by the developing countries today are unprecedented in history. Because of the ever-growing interdependency of the countries of the world, problems are of concern to the developed nations as well. If, in fact, there is a trade-off between growth and equity, the prospects for solving the problems are bleak, for redistributing today's income will only make tomorrow's problem worse. If the trade-off can be avoided, then there is some cause for hope. Whether the problems can best be faced by focusing on improving the functioning of markets in general or by focusing on policies which serve to increase the proportion of wealth in the hands of the poor, or most likely, some combination of these (since they are by no means independent), is an unsettled question. But at least there are some positive and hopeful alternatives available.

NOTES

1. The political unrest and eventual downfall of the Ayub Khan government in the late 1960s in Pakistan is often contrasted with the relative stability of India. During the 1960s the Pakistan economy grew more rapidly than that of India. The degree of inequality of distribution grew in Pakistan, however, whereas in India the political rhetoric suggests that inequality was reduced. This experience indicates that the degree of equality, at least as perceived by the majority, is more important than growth *per se*.

2. See James W. Land and Ronald Soligo, "Income Distribution, Employment, and Growth in Labor Redundant Economies," Program of Development Studies Discussion Paper no. 9, Rice University, 1971.

3. Because of the index number problem it is not possible to say unambiguously that output increases. Measured in base period prices, however, aggregate output is higher after the income transfer.

4. See International Labour Office, *Towards Full Employment: A Programme for Colombia* (Geneva: International Labour Organization, 1970), pp. 127-136; and Hollis Chenery, Montek S. Ahluwalia, C. L. G. Bell, John H. Duloy, and Richard Jolly, *Redistribution with Growth* (London: Oxford University Press, 1974).

5. Much of this work has been summarized by Soligo in "Consumption Patterns, Factor Usage and the Distribution of Income: A Review of Some Findings," paper presented at the Southern Economic Association Meetings in Atlanta, Georgia, November 1971.

6. Interesting qualifications to this statement arise when one considers the capital and labor required to produce capital goods in addition to what is required to produce consumer goods. This point is discussed at some length in Ronald Soligo, "Factor Intensity of Consumption Patterns, Income Distribution and Employment Growth in Pakistan," Program of Development Studies Discussion Paper 44 (1973), and in "Consumption Patterns, Factor Usage and the Distribution of Income: A Review of Some Findings."

7. For recent surveys of the literature see Raymond F. Mikesell and James E. Zinser, "The Nature of the Savings Function in Developing Countries: A Survey of the Theoretical and Empirical Literature," *Journal of Economic Literature* **5** (March 1973): 1-26; and Robert Ferber, "Consumer Economics, A Survey," *Journal of Economic Literature* **11** (December 1973): 1302-42.

AGRICULTURAL POLICY AND INCOME DISTRIBUTION IN COLOMBIA

by Wayne R. Thirsk

I. INTRODUCTION

Making the distribution of income less unequal and achieving higher levels of total output per capita are two of the major goals of economic performance in less developed countries. However desirable these ambitions might be, an enormous volume of literature in economics has stressed that simultaneous satisfaction of both goals may not be possible. There may be a basic incompatibility between these objectives of economic policy if higher output levels require greater income inequality or if measures which provide more equal incomes also produce reductions in total income.

Empirical work by Simon Kuznets has confirmed that in the early stages of economic development and sustained growth the distribution of income appears to widen markedly.[1] Only at a much later stage of development is there a change towards less inequality in incomes earned. Although the discovery of initial divergence and later convergence in income distribution has aroused considerable speculation and curiosity on the part of economists, only very tentative explanations for it have been advanced so far. Most of these refer to the relative abundance of labor in the early stages and the positive role an unequal income distribution plays in promoting saving and capital accumulation, which will eventually make labor a scarce factor of production. Although it is imperfectly understood, Kuznets's observation is widely accepted as almost an immutable law of economic development and growth.

Reaction to the constraints imposed on economic policy by the apparent trade-off in economic goals has frequently involved attaching greater weight to one or the other of them. Some groups now draw a distinction between growth and development and argue that the latter requires raising the relative income of the very poor regardless of the growth rate achieved. They are prepared to accept slower growth rates of output in pursuing the income distribution objective. Others reject this position in favor of growth-promoting strategies and see the distributional issue as posing a challenge to the flexi-

Mr. Thirsk is Assistant Professor of Economics at the University of Manitoba.

bility of fiscal policy. They would rely on a variety of fiscal measures to redistribute market incomes to lower income groups as the best means of reconciling the conflict in objectives. Groups with above average incomes who benefit in particular from economic growth would be taxed to finance income transfers and government expenditures that aid low income members of the economy.

While there may be a great deal of truth to the conflict notion as a broad description of development trends, it is probably dangerous and misleading to view it as inevitable in the context of specific policies affecting particular sectors of the economy. In Latin America, policies to promote and accelerate the process of economic growth have typically relied upon import substitution efforts and rigorous governmental influence in the sectoral distribution of resources. Colombia's recent economic experience is ample testimony of such broad governmental impact. Government policy in that country is the dominant force in the setting of foreign exchange and interest rates, the variety of effective tax and subsidy rates for different firms and industries, minimum wage regulations, tariffs, and quantitative trade restrictions. In short, there is a wide panoply of laws regulating many kinds of market transactions. In affecting the terms under which different economic groups and sectors may have access to resources, these restrictions frequently distort the use of resources and prevent their efficient allocation in the economy as a whole. Economists traditionally have been intrigued with describing and measuring the loss in economic efficiency or the welfare cost of this kind of policy discrimination. Only recently has much attention been devoted to the consequences these actions may have for income distribution. Since they normally work to raise the relative price of abundant factors (especially labor) and thus reduce demand for them, it is becoming increasingly recognized and accepted that these policies accentuate inequalities in income. If this is true, a shift in existing government policy may be able to achieve both a higher level of total output and less inequality in income distribution. It may lie within relatively easy reach of governments in less developed countries to eliminate much of the competitive relationship between growth and income distribution and to impose a stronger complementarity between these goals.

In what follows there is a review and discussion of some research seeking to assess the efficiency and equity aspects of some major government policies that are important in influencing the direction of development in Colombia's agricultural sector.[2] These policies consist of measures to affect the distribution of physical capital resources through land reform and subsidies to large farm purchase of capital goods (mechanization) and the distribution of human capital in the form of access to educational opportunities. In addition, there are rural credit policies which affect the pattern of use of variable production inputs such as seed and fertilizer, and agricultural price support policies, which determine the returns farmers receive from the sale of output. In each of these five policy areas some empirical evidence is marshaled to see whether it offers any support for the basic hypothesis that a reconstruction of existing policies could both equalize the distribution and raise the level of total income. With but one possible exception, subsequent sections strongly suggest that a transfer of real resources to smaller farms and less policy favoritism towards larger ones would be not only equitable but efficient as well.

II. AGRICULTURAL PRICE SUPPORTS

As in many countries, Colombia's experience with agricultural price supports originated in the depression of the 1930s in response to severe balance of payments difficulties. Thereafter, price supports became part of an overall import substitution strategy of economic development in which the agency responsible for setting and maintaining domestic price levels sought to achieve self-sufficiency in agricultural production. This agency relied on its nearly exclusive right to import agricultural commodities under a system of foreign exchange licensing in order to validate its system of price supports. Levels of support were determined annually on the basis of estimates of the average cost of domestic production, including a normal rate of return on investment.

Because it is privileged to buy crops at world prices and sell at higher domestic prices and, to a lesser extent, because its normal price-stabilizing activities require buying low and selling dear, the price support agency earns trading profits that are used to finance the costs of operation and the costs of storage. Supply adjustments from crop inventories and imports provide the agency with ample leverage for controlling the movement of domestic prices. Except for wheat, which remains a sizable import item, the agency has been successful in reducing dependence on foreign sources of supply for a large number of crops. The price paid for greater autarky (economic self-sufficiency) is a structure of domestic crop production whose costs of output in many cases are substantially above world price levels. Some portion of this cost difference is attributable to persistent over-valuation of the Colombian peso, which artificially depresses the foreign exchange cost of imports. Moreover, in the case of one crop, cotton, an import substitution phase was soon followed by an export phase as the country acquired sufficient experience in growing the crop to be able to sell it in world markets without price assistance. For some crops, supply has shown a consistent tendency to outpace growth in demand, with a consequent accumulation of unsold output that eventually has been sold abroad at a loss. For example, in 1969 corn and rice inventories bulged and were reduced to more manageable size by sale to foreigners with the aid of a budgetary subsidy worth 32.5 million pesos (about 1.82 million dollars). In the presence of an overvalued exchange rate, however, there is a strong resource allocation argument for export subsidies, one form of which is the losses sustained by a government marketing agency. Export losses would be inappropriate only if the implicit subsidy on export sales exceeded the extent of the overvaluation.

In analyzing the income distribution consequences of this price support program, consideration is given both to how different income groups earn their income and to how they spend it. This approach has the advantage of focusing on the change in the real income position of any income group that is produced by a change in price support policy. Previous studies have ignored the expenditure side of household accounts and have concentrated exclusively on how various programs affect the nominal earnings or income of farmers.[3] The methodology adopted for Colombia obliterates the distinction between rural and urban members of an income class and emphasizes redistribution among income classes regardless of the sector of the economy in which members of any class work or reside.[4] While it offers a desirably broad perspective on the redistribution question, the methodology neglects significant redistribution within income classes in order to emphasize that occurring between income classes.

Another important methodological matter revolves around the appropriate counterfactual situation. If the price support program were abandoned, what price situation would prevail in its absence? The simplest situation would be one in which domestic crop prices fell to world price levels. If this occurred, there would be much greater demand for imported crop commodities and consequent upward pressure on the exchange rate. Under these circumstances a meaningful price comparison would be with existing world price levels adjusted for depreciation of the Colombian peso. Since the extent of any depreciation is unknown, an interesting and policy-relevant base for comparison is the structure of world prices that would rule if the current overvaluation of the peso were removed. This would involve augmenting world prices by approximately 30-35%, which many economists judge to be a rough order of magnitude of the current overvaluation. In any event, without a fully specified model of the economy it is important to account for as many relative price changes as possible in comparing actual and hypothetical income distributions.

With the aid of an input-output model of the Colombian economy, it was possible to partition the agricultural sector into five income classes and eight price-supported crops, showing how much each income group spent on each crop and how much it earned in producing the crop. For each crop the data indicated that another dollar added to the price of the crop would cause larger increases in expenditures than in earnings for the low income groups and greater additions to earnings than to expenditures for the high income groups. Because the poor invariably spend more on any crop than they earn in producing it and the reverse situation applies for the rich, eliminating the system of price supports would redistribute income from rich to poor in most cases. Only for rice and barley, in which cases adjusted world prices equal domestic market prices, would the rich-to-poor redistribution fail to occur. For one crop, beans, the income transfers would move the other way, because adjusted world prices exceed observed market prices. Because wheat is a large import item, all consumers and income classes, but especially lower ones, would benefit if price supports for it were removed. To put these results in a somewhat different light, continuation of the present program of price supports implies a continuous redistribution of income from poor to rich. The real burden of price supports is borne disproportionately by low-income consumers, while most of the benefits accrue to high-income producers.

An alternative way of viewing the matter is to examine changes in the functional distribution of income between owners of land and "owners" of labor. As a result of inelastic final demand, price supports raise the amount of total revenue to be divided between land and labor. Since labor is readily available in the agricultural sector and land is in relatively fixed supply, the impact of higher product prices will be felt in the form of higher returns to, and a larger income share for, the land input. As the ownership of land is much more highly concentrated than the ownership of labor, a higher income share for land implies more inequality in the distribution of personal incomes. Seen from another angle, the least labor-intensive farms stand to gain the most from price supports, and these farms comprise the larger ones with higher initial incomes.

In addition to redistributing income, price supports impair the overall efficiency of resource allocation in the economy. The size of the efficiency cost is indicated by the discrepancy between domestic crop prices and adjusted world prices. This price margin measures, under a reasonably nonrestrictive set of assumptions, the extra resource cost of producing a commodity domestically rather than purchasing it indirectly through the sale of exports abroad. The extra cost is the price paid for pursuing the goal of self-sufficiency and failing to specialize production according to the free trade concept of comparative advantage. For wheat, soybeans, and corn, the cost of diversification was estimated to be about 5% of the total domestic value of output. With respect to the total value of all crop output, it would be an even smaller percentage. It seems safe to conclude that the efficiency cost of the price support program is not unreasonably high, although it is a cost which is paid with no offsetting benefit of a less skewed income distribution.

III. AGRICULTURAL CREDIT

Credit is an important means by which farmers acquire command over the use of productive inputs such as seeds, fertilizer, pesticides, and farm machinery. The use of credit to purchase large and indivisible, multi-period resources in the form of farm machinery and equipment is examined in the next section of this paper. Here attention is concentrated on how the credit-financed allocation of intermediate inputs, essentially seed, fertilizer, and irrigation, affects the distribution of farm incomes. There are many facets to this issue and only some of the myriad channels by which credit influences distribution have been subjected to empirical testing. In general, income distribution will be affected by who receives the credit or the size and kind of farm on which it is used, the price paid for its use, the productivity of the inputs financed by credit, and the particular type of input purchased. Each of these matters is discussed in turn in the context of Colombia's credit markets.

The price paid for institutional credit in Colombia is regulated by government at artificially low interest rates. About one quarter of Colombian farmers receive credit from some type of institutional lender. The semi-official agricultural bank, the Caja Agraria, accounts for slightly more than one half of the outstanding loans to agriculture, most of which have gone to relatively large farmers. Private banks likewise bias their lending activities in the direction of large farmers. The single source of institutional finance for smaller farmers is the supervised credit program of the land reform institute, which has accounted for about 5% of total loans outstanding and has benefited perhaps 35,000 families during the period 1964-1972. This is a small fraction of the approximately 850,000 small farmers (those controlling fewer than five hectares) who produce about 20% of all crops and 15% of all livestock.

A prominent characteristic of the credit market is a system of obligatory investments imposed on financial institutions for the purpose of controlling the allocation of credit to specific sectors. For example, private banks are legally required to set aside 15% of their deposits for agricultural loans. Credit controls of this and similar types are needed to force funds to flow toward agricultural activities paying lower loan rates than those charged in the non-agricultural sector. These controls have succeeded in siphoning off a growing share of total loan capacity for agriculture. Currently agriculture owes about 35% of total loans outstanding, compared to its share in Gross Domestic Product of about 30%.

Maintaining low nominal and real rates of interest has several implications for income distribution. Low real rates of interest typically generate an excess demand for loans and force lenders to ration their lending capacity. In deciding on who is to receive credit, lenders will not be influenced by the productivity of the loan, since this is not reflected in the rate paid by the borrower, and will instead be swayed by other considerations, such as the credit-worthiness of the borrower. By choosing this loan strategy the lender is protected against risk of default, but the result is an institutional bias in favor of large landowners who control more net worth. Through access to cheap lines of credit there may be an income transfer to wealthy borrowers from poor savers who do not have alternative outlets for their savings. In addition, many high yielding investment projects on small farms may go unrealized for lack of financing. As long as the return on the use of credit exceeds its cost, the allocation of more credit to small farmers represents a transfer of income-earning resources to them. If this credit is instead allocated to large farmers, they may use it to finance new capital-intensive technologies which diminish the demand for labor, including that of small farmers, and to increase their output levels, thereby reducing the prices small farmers receive for their output. Regardless of who receives the credit, if it is productive and augments total output, consumers (particularly poor ones who spend most of their income on food), will share in the increase in output by being able to purchase at lower prices.

There are two other less obvious links between credit allocation and income distribution. First, the use of credit to promote growth in output of particular crops and to alter the overall composition of crop output will have an effect on income distribution depending on the labor intensity of different crops. For example, fertilizer could be competitive with the employment of labor if it has a high payoff in stimulating advances in the output of land-using, labor-saving crops. Secondly, the distribution of credit between large and small farmers may have serious consequences for the distribution of incomes between small farmers and landless workers. A larger share of credit garnered by small farmers that have surplus labor capacity may harm landless workers to the extent that small farmers hire less labor per dollar of credit than do larger farms. Opposing any such tendency, however, would be the withdrawal of labor services from the labor market by small farmers, so that the net effect on landless labor is in doubt.

Because of exclusionary credit market practices that may restrict their opportunity to purchase intermediate inputs such as seed and fertilizer, the marginal productivity of these inputs may be highest on smaller farms in Colombia. The relative abundance of complementary labor on these farms also works in the same direction. A limited test of this hypothesis was performed with the aid of statistical production function analysis which permitted the estimation of marginal products on different sized farms. The test was limited by the available data on credit use, which described only a narrow range of fairly small farm sizes and which did not readily allow inferences to be drawn about the productivity of intermediate inputs on much larger farms. There is some evidence, however, that larger farms utilize even greater amounts of credit per hectare than is suggested by the sample data. In this case the statistical results will admit of some broad, if somewhat tenuous, generalization. For what they are worth, the results of the production function analysis indicated that in six of twelve cases (crop-region combinations) the marginal productivity of credit was significantly higher on smaller farms. In another four cases the estimated marginal productivity was also higher on smaller farms but the difference was insufficiently large to be significant at the 95% confidence level. These findings receive corroboration from some independent studies of Brazil, which discovered that the financial system directed a much higher fraction of credit to large farms displaying inferior productivity. It is possible that the results for Colombia illustrate a deficiency in the supply of long-term credit for the acquisition of land. No lending institution in Colombia provides financing for this purpose. Perhaps intermediate inputs are more productive on smaller farms because they substitute for land purchases that would otherwise be made. Nonetheless, for a number of crops and regions a reallocation of credit based on productivity criteria appears to offer some scope for reducing income inequality.

IV. FARM MECHANIZATION

Since the late 1940s the use of tractors and other farm machinery in Colombia has grown at close to an annual rate of 20%, so that by 1964 mechanized crop production accounted for almost 50% of total crop output (excluding coffee). Over the same period real wages in the rural sector displayed a barely perceptible rate of growth. The stimulus to mechanization has had its origins not so much in increasing labor scarcity as in government policies which have cheapened the cost of farm machinery. Both interest rates charged by lenders and empirical estimates of the rate of return to capital indicate that users of farm capital enjoy a subsidy relative to capital users in other parts of the economy. If the subsidy is measured as a fraction of either the rate of return or the cost of capital in non-agricultural activities, it is of the order of about 40%. In addition, farm machinery receives favorable tax treatment in that it is exempt from the wealth tax and faces a much lower tariff (2%) than is levied on other imports of capital goods.

Colombia's agricultural sector is composed of two distinct subsectors, a large farm group producing either crops or cattle and a collection of much smaller farms specializing in various crops. For any given crop, small farms are observed to use a great deal more labor per hectare than larger farms. Between very small crop farms and large cattle ranches as much as ten to fifteen times more labor per unit of land is used on the former than on the latter. The wide variation in factor proportions reflects different technological choices in addition to different products. Larger farms producing any crop employ higher ratios of machinery to labor. According to the 1960 census of agriculture, nearly 70% of all tractors were owned on farms of more than fifty hectares and, although small farmers tend to rent machinery services from larger farms, there is still a wide discrepancy in the use of farm machinery by farm size. From the same census data it has been estimated that the use of tractor horsepower per unit of labor increases by about 12% for every 10% increment in farm size.

Given the opportunity of small farmers to rent machinery services, the evidence suggests that small farmers may value their own, or their family's, labor services at something less than the price large farmers pay for labor. Since the value that small farmers place on their own labor is likely to correspond more closely to the real cost to the economy of using labor than does the market wage, the concentration of farm machinery on large farms suggests that rural labor markets do not function well in allocating resources. Small farmer demands for machinery services are significantly less than those of larger farmers and are of a much more selective nature. When they hire the services of farm machinery, small farmers appear to use it almost exclusively for land preparation. Since this operation is crucial to improved yield performance and is more difficult or costly to perform with either human or animal labor, it may prove useful to confine mechanization to the land preparation phase with the aim of achieving a significant output gain at a relatively small cost in lost employment.

From a sample of individual farms it is possible to put together a picture of the input ratios found on large-scale mechanized operations. Farms in this class appear to use about 1-1.4 tractor horsepower per cultivated hectare, 7.5-8 tractor horsepower per man-year of employment, and, averaging over the different labor requirements for cotton, rice, and corn, about 35-40 man-days per hectare. Comparing these input demands to those on unmechanized farms at the same output level and holding other aspects of farm technology constant, the transition towards mechanized farm operations appears to result in a labor saving of about 50% for most crops. In other words, a 50-60 horsepower tractor with a full complement of field equipment probably replaces the services of from six to eight farm workers.

A more refined substitution ratio, using service flows instead of stocks of men and machinery, indicates that a single tractor hour can replace, depending on the specific operation or task involved, somewhere between three and five man-days. Substitution rates of this magnitude were not necessarily realized in Colombia because in many instances mechanization was associated with a change in output composition whereby land use was switched from cattle to crops. Since cattle raising uses even less labor than mechanized crops require (approximately fifteen man-days per hectare in most regions), the diffusion of mechanical technology among large farms probably resulted in an increase in labor demand. Another facet of Colombian experience, however, is that the subsidy to the use of farm machinery has been applied to a sector which is more capital-intensive than the non-agricultural sector as a whole. It is this aspect of the subsidy which is largely responsible for the negative impact mechanization has had on employment and income equalization.

To understand this result, consider a qualitative description of some of the economic adjustments that follow in the wake of granting a capital subsidy to large farms. At existing crop prices, large farmers will find it profitable to increase their planned levels of production as a result of diminished production costs. Higher output levels will be translated into lower crop prices in agricultural product markets. Lower priced capital will be substituted for labor and will stimulate a demand for the complementary input of mechanizable land. Cattle ranches will supply the new demand for land. Ranchers will relinquish control of some mechanizable land and substitute land less suitable for mechanization in its stead. As some land is bid away from cattle and transferred to crops, its relative price will rise, moderating the demand for capital and encouraging greater use of labor on large crop farms. With the higher price of land, the relative price of cattle will be greater than before and will elicit still greater consumer demand for crops. The shift in the composition of output will augment the demand for labor, since crop production employs more labor per hectare than does cattle raising.

The non-agricultural sector will find that capital otherwise supplied to it will be diverted instead to the capital-intensive large farm crop sector. With less capital, the rate of return earned on capital in the non-agricultural sector will increase. The higher price of capital will lead to higher output prices for the non-agricultural sector and will shift more consumer spending to crops and cattle. Because non-agricultural activities are on average more labor-intensive than large farm crops, the alteration in output mix will be associated with a reduction in labor demand. Offsetting this tendency is the very tight linkage between money wage rates and the prices of crop output. For unskilled labor, money wage rates deflated by the price of crop goods display virtual stability over the post-war period. When crop prices decline, money wages would be expected to follow suit, occasioning a greater demand for cheaper labor in all parts of the non-agricultural sector. How income distribution is affected by these product and factor market adjustments will depend on the relative size and strength of the various repercussions. On the face of it, owners of capital and land appear to benefit from the resulting increase in the price of capital and the return to mechanizable land. Labor may also stand to gain, however, if it is able to escape the low incomes earned on small farms by finding employment in other higher paying sectors where labor demand rises.

To sort these matters out more finely it seems there is no alternative to more rigorous quantitative analysis. Elsewhere I have constructed a small general equilibrium model of the Colombian economy and used it to simulate the employment and relative price effects of subsidized farm mechanization.[5] The simulations proved to be reasonably robust in the sense that most of the results were little affected by alternative assumptions about the appropriate size of different parameters. For every simulation there was a significant increase in the utilization of all of the inputs employed by large crop farms: capital, land, and labor as well. The number of people occupied on small farms—where labor is assumed to go if employment cannot be obtained in other sectors—depended crucially on the ability of non-agricultural sectors to absorb more labor when the price of labor relative to the price of non-agricultural goods was reduced. Capital/labor ratios invariably rose in large farm crop operations and fell in the other sectors outside agriculture. Without exception the prices paid for land, capital, and non-agricultural goods increased relative to the price of labor.

Overall the predictions of the simulation model appeared to mirror the trend of observable events in Colombia reasonably well: fast rates of growth of mechanized crop output and of all the inputs used in this sector; disappointing employment growth in non-agricultural sectors (though mechanization is only partially responsible for this result); a switch of some level, productive land from cattle to crops; increased labor productivity in mechanized crops coupled with steady or declining labor productivity in small farm operations; modest deterioration in the relative price of crops, and a higher relative price for the service of land.

One of the more interesting results is the strong possibility that greater labor employment on large crop farms can coincide with diminished employment prospects for small farmers, even though the shift in output from cattle to crops will increase labor demand. The explanation for this result is that reduced employment opportunities in non-agricultural activities may overwhelm the expansion of employment on large crop farms. Despite the induced movement to a greater labor/output ratio in non-agriculture, total employment in this sector may well be less, due to a lower level of output.

After specifying how different functional income groups spend their income on crops, cattle, and non-agricultural goods, the simulation results were used to make an explicit calculation of the income redistribution implied by an altered pattern of relative prices. These calculations for alternative simulations uniformly produced the result that capital owners were the primary beneficiaries of the subsidy to mechanization. At least three quarters of their gain in real income was realized at the expense of workers and small farmers, who experienced reductions in their real incomes. Small farmers became worse off on two accounts. First, mechanization reduced the prices they received for the sale of their output and, in addition, the total demand for their labor services was reduced.[6] The latter effect by itself could depress the average income earned by small farmers by between five and ten percent.

Combining all sources of non-labor income, the analytic evidence strongly points to the finding that subsidized farm mechanization has had the effect of producing more pronounced inequality in the distribution of income, which would show a highly skewed pattern even without policies to promote greater farm mechanization.

There remains the question of determining how the progress of mechanization has affected the overall efficiency of resource allocation. Here a number of offsetting influences are at work. It is alleged that there is an external benefit associated with mechanization in the form of a reallocation of land from low productivity use in raising cattle to higher productivity uses in growing crops. Scattered empirical evidence available seems to support this claim. Thus while mechanization may make the allocation of labor and capital resources less efficient, the loss in efficiency may be more than offset by a more efficient allocation of land. The net outcome of these conflicting forces is indeterminate without further information, since everything depends on the size of the various factor market distortions and the extent to which mechanization changes the allocation of different resources.

From the results of the simulation's estimates of resource reallocation, it was found that the gains in total output ensuing from a better distribution of land were insufficient to outweigh the losses in total output attributable to a worse allocation of capital and labor. The welfare cost of the net loss in real income was less than 1% of gross national product in all cases. It is open to some debate whether or not losses of this magnitude should be considered relevant for policy making. One percent of gross national product is still a significant sum in absolute terms and indicates the absence of a socially profitable investment. Since external lenders have underwritten a large fraction of the cost of mechanization in Colombia, however, the welfare loss arises only in comparison with a neutral subsidy policy which did not offer any special incentives to the sectoral employment of capital. It is not so much that total real income has declined in response to mechanization policy as that it could have been higher without the discriminatory inducement to use more capital on large crop farms.

A summary judgment of the Colombian experience with mechanization would be that it has been an unfortunate investment with little to recommend it. It has yielded a negative social payoff and has acted to increase income inequality in a country which already had a highly skewed distribution of income before the investment took place. Elimination of the subsidy to mechanization should have the twofold benefit of equalizing income distribution and augmenting the level of total income. Removal of subsidy could be effected by the levying of a tax on purchases of capital for large farms or by the imposition of higher interest rate charges on the loans granted to buyers of capital used on large farms.

V. LAND REFORM

Although a measure of land reform occurred in the middle 1930s, it was not until 1961 that Colombia began serious efforts to increase the land base of small farmers. A creature of the comprehensive agrarian reform law of 1961 was a new land reform institute, INCORA, which was vested with broad discretionary powers and multiple functions. INCORA was empowered to assist Colombia's numerous and impoverished small farmers through infrastructural investment in remote colonization areas, irrigation and drainage projects, a supervised credit program, and, finally, through distribution of land in the public domain as well as of private land acquired by gift, voluntary sale, or expropriation. With so many options from which to choose, INCORA has been characterized as more nearly resembling a rural development agency than a vehicle for substantial modification of land tenure conditions. To some, the multi-faceted nature of INCORA is lamentable, since other activities may be used as a substitute for land redistribution and may provide an excuse for diversion of its administrative energies and financial capacities.

Among many distributive issues that might be considered, three have been singled out for discussion below. Could INCORA have been more effective in achieving its goals given the resources that were committed to it (INCORA receives about 20% of the total resources invested in agriculture from public revenue)? Will landless workers be helped or harmed by the efforts to improve income prospects for small farmers? What is the size of the gain in total agricultural output that a full-scale reform would bring, and what would be the division between land beneficiaries and urban consumers?

From an income distribution point of view, it is important that INCORA be guided by efficiency considerations in choosing among projects related to land acquisition, land improvement, and land extension (colonization). The distribution impact of a fixed INCORA budget will be greatest if the funds are allocated to the least costly methods of helping a poor rural family reach a particular income level. At current land prices it appears to cost less (per family settled at a given income) to acquire land by outright purchase than to engage in relatively more expensive irrigation and drainage programs. Colonization projects appear to cost even more since they require the provision of infrastructure which is already at least partially available in more settled parts of the country. If present cost estimates are valid, they suggest that INCORA could make more small farmers better off by spending more of its budget on large farm land acquisition and less on irrigation and colonization projects.

It is a somewhat puzzling feature of land reform programs that they do not extend to landless workers who are often at the bottom of the income scale. In Colombia the approximately 10% of rural workers who are virtually without any land have never been considered as a target group for land reform activities. If small farmers have surplus family labor prior to reform, they may employ smaller amounts of hired labor on land transferred to them by reform than the former owners employed on the same land. Thus a change in the pattern of land ownership in favor of small farmers may result in a displacement of landless workers whose wages, employment, or both, would decline.[7] If this were to occur, land reform would have an ambiguous effect on income distribution, as incomes of small farmers would be enhanced at the combined expense of richer large farmers and poor landless workers. Whether this is a likely outcome is an empirical matter which depends in part on the size of the land reform parcel. For very small sizes, the demand for landless labor may be reduced as the land is used to employ family members more fully. Drawing on data from farm level analysis, it appears that small farms employ somewhat more hired labor per hectare than larger farms producing the same crop in a given region. The main reason for this result is that small farms engage in the production of relatively labor-intensive commodities, and, compared to large farms, do not rely on labor-saving methods of production. This evidence indicates that landless workers will not be harmed by land reform and could conceivably be in greater demand if the large expropriated farms had specialized in crops with low labor intensity.

A characteristic of Colombian agriculture is that larger farms tend to cultivate a smaller fraction of their land and operate with larger amounts of fallow than do small farms. Even though larger farms may enjoy higher yields on cultivated land, output per unit of total land area declines appreciably with increasing farm size. By combining underutilized land from large farms with underutilized labor from small farms, land reform should increase the level of total agricultural output. A more even distribution of labor than at present, and perhaps other variable inputs as well, over a given area of cultivated land, will have the same effect of raising total output. Estimates of this output contribution of land reform point to an increase on the order of about ten to fifteen percent. Urban food consumers, particularly low income ones, would share in this output benefit if marketed farm output also rose and relative food prices therefore declined. Estimates of the induced demand for food by small farmers, however, indicates that they will tend to capture all of the benefit from the gain in output. One cannot rule out the possibility that total marketed output will decline absolutely and reduce the real incomes of urban consumers of food. In fact, the poorer the land reform beneficiaries are, the greater is the probability of a smaller marketed output (because the owners themselves consume more), and the greater the prospect of harming the urban poor.

Many factors responsible for widely disparate rural incomes are in the end related to the skewed distribution of land ownership. A socially inefficient process of large farm mechanization would not have occurred if the initial distribution of land had been more equal. Moreover, deficiencies in the supply of rural education probably would have been remedied long ago if large landowners had resided on their farms and sent their children to local schools. Finally, price support policies would have a much less inequitable impact if they did not provide disproportionate rewards to some simply because they own more land and have more to sell than others. It is in this sense that land reform is the fundamental element in improving income distribution. Without it, many other policies affecting the rural sector make the distribution of income more unequal than it otherwise would be.

VI. RURAL EDUCATION

Two salient characteristics of the Colombian educational system are, first, the steadily growing participation at all levels of the population in the eligible age groups and, secondly, a marked disparity in educational opportunity between the rural and urban sectors of the economy in favor of the latter. Since the end of World War II, enrollments at every educational level have been increasing faster than the rate of population growth. Hidden in the aggregate numbers, however, is a significant difference in the educational distributions for rural and urban groups. Compared to urban areas, rural zones suffer severely limited access to education. The percentage of school-aged children (under fifteen years) attending rural schools is about one-half as high as in the cities. In 1964 more than two-thirds of rural schools offered instruction only through the second grade, while almost all the others went up only to the third grade. In contrast, 62% of urban schools provided the full five years of primary school. Moreover, less than 10% of secondary schools are located in rural areas.

Greater equality in educational opportunity would be expected under most conditions to generate a reduction in the inequality of labor incomes. Since the poor tend to participate in the Colombian educational system only at the primary level, an expansion of primary school enrollments, especially in rural areas, should produce greater income equality. Conversely, if university and secondary education were expanded instead, middle and upper income groups would benefit disproportionately, with the result of a more unequal distribution of labor incomes. In a country where political power is concentrated in the hands of the rich, one might expect educational spending to under-invest in primary education benefiting the masses and to over-invest in higher education primarily benefiting the rich. Empirical studies of the rate of return to education in Colombia indicate the existence of such an investment pattern in urban localities.[8] The rate of return for urban primary schooling appears to be substantially higher than that for university education and well in excess of estimates of the opportunity cost of capital in the economy. In short, urban primary schooling is a profitable social investment, and considerations of economic efficiency would dictate larger expenditures for the education of the urban poor, which would raise their expected future incomes relative to the rest of the population.

No data or study exists which would permit this conclusion to be extrapolated to the rural sector. Perhaps the most that can be said with current knowledge is that rural primary schooling will be a worthwhile investment if it equips students with the skills needed to obtain and hold urban jobs. One study hints of a basic conflict between equity and efficiency in the provision of rural education.[9] It found that rural education had a significant payoff only in the rich, well-endowed regions of the country. In those areas primary education assisted small farmers in making more profitable production decisions because the correct production choice could result in much larger profits. In the poorer regions of the country, growth in output is severely constrained by adverse topography and poor soils which cannot be altered or offset by farmers' production decisions. The problem is that education seems to be complementary to inputs that are either missing or in deficient supply on farms in the poorest regions. Without them more education may not be helpful.

VII. SUMMARY

Agricultural price supports, land reform, credit allocation, farm mechanization, and rural education comprise a diverse set of policies whose analysis would not ordinarily share a single theme. My review of research in these separate areas has attempted to show that a more equal distribution of income in Colombian agriculture is not inconsistent with the achievement of higher levels of output. In most areas of policymaking there is some scope for better performance with regard to both equity and economic efficiency. In many cases what is required to achieve this end is an adjustment in current agricultural policies so as to give small farmers improved opportunities to acquire productive inputs and to remove from large farmers their privileged access to the same resources. If this were to happen the distinction between economic growth and development probably would no longer have to be made in describing the changes in the behavior of Colombian agriculture. Finally, a policy adjustment in the direction indicated would have the desirable effect of raising the demand for rural labor, increasing rural incomes, and thus of limiting the tide of rural-to-urban migration to a level that the cities could absorb without severe economic stress and dislocation.

NOTES

1. S. Kuznets, "Economic Growth and Income Inequality," *American Economic Review* **45**, no. 1 (March 1955):1-28.

2. A more complete description of this research is contained in the following discussion papers by Wayne R. Thirsk in the Rice University Program of Development Studies series: No. 33, "Income Distribution, Efficiency and the Experience of Colombian Farm Mechanization," 1972; No. 43, "Income Distribution Consequences of Agricultural Price Supports in Colombia," 1973; No. 51, "Rural Credit and Income Distribution in Colombia," 1974; No. 53, "Some Aspects of Efficiency and Income Distribution in Colombian Land Reform," 1974 (mimeograph).

3. See, for example, James T. Bonnen, "The Distribution of Benefits from Selected U.S. Farm Programs," *Rural Poverty in the United States: A Report of the President's National Advisory Commission on Rural Poverty* (Washington, D.C., 1968); Charles L. Schultze, *The Distribution of Farm Subsidies* (Washington, D.C.: The Brookings Institution, 1971).

4. Recent grumblings over the effect on food prices of the U.S. wheat sale to Russia illustrate the dangers involved in overlooking the expenditure side of household budgets. The U.S. Department of Agriculture, which engineered the sale, was concerned only with improving nominal farm incomes.

5. W. R. Thirsk, "The Economics of Colombian Farm Mechanization," unpublished Ph.D. dissertation, Yale University, 1972.

6. The model abstracts from the possibility that domestic production may be exported on world markets or be used to replace imports of crop goods. Except for cotton Colombia has not penetrated the world market for exports, and wheat is the only crop in which Colombia has not achieved virtual self-sufficiency.

If domestic prices were determined by world prices, the prices received by small farmers would not decline as production of large farm crops increased. Real wages earned in the non-agricultural sectors also would not decline, however, so that demand for small farm labor services would be even less under these conditions. If the expansion of large farm crop production either earns or saves foreign exchange, the investment capacity of the non-agricultural sector may be enlarged. If this were to happen, total labor demand would increase, making the smaller farmers better off. Through the channel of international trade it is feasible to establish a complementary, rather than competitive, linkage between investment in the agricultural and non-agricultural sectors. It is for precisely these reasons that mechanization of a crop on the margin of exportability may be a sound investment.

7. For a more complete analysis see R. Albert Berry, "Land Reform and Agricultural Income Distribution," *Pakistan Development Review* **11** (Spring 1971):30-44.

8. These studies are by T. P. Schultz, *Returns to Education in Bogotá, Colombia* (Santa Monica, Calif.: The Rand Corporation, 1968); and M. Selowsky, "The Effect of Unemployment and Growth on the Rate of Return to Education: The Case of Colombia," Harvard University Development Advisory Service, Economic Development Report No. 116 (November 1968).

9. Tom Haller, "Education and Rural Development in Colombia," unpublished Ph.D. dissertation, Purdue University, 1972.

LOW INCOME HOUSING DEVELOPMENT IN BOGOTA

by Stephen O. Bender

I. INTRODUCTION

Patrick Geddes wrote in 1918, "I have to remind all concerned: 1) that the essential need of a house and family is *room*, and 2) that the essential improvement of a house and family is *more room*."[1] While written for another place, the statement is still timely if we are to examine in some detail the growth and development of low income settlements in Latin American urban settings. The traditional analysis of the growth of such settlements, usually in sociopolitical and economic terms, has left us with an array of classifications by which to understand one of the most significant occurrences in the history of man's urbanization. Such analysis has allowed us to describe in some detail the extent to which low income families, often migrant in origin, have sought to resolve their housing needs outside accepted norms, and to scrutinize the efforts of the public sector to aid in (if not to control) the housing of these poor. The preceding type of analysis has brought into focus the dissimilarities between housing built and maintained by its inhabitants and housing provided through government intervention.

Critical to the understanding of settlements, however, is an analysis of the commonalities of low income housing development and, more specifically, the physical characteristics which over time make settlements of various legal origins indistinguishable from one another. "That the mass of people demand no more than they can economically support is the existence of the squatter settlement"[2] is not only applicable to clandestine developments, but also appropriate to all low income housing development. Low income families continually match available resources with existing needs and over a period of time change simple shelters into a community with a full complement of services.

The role this housing development plays and some of the economic opportunities it presents are examined in this paper. In summary, traditional views of squatter settlement development, those built outside of accepted

Mr. Bender is an Adjunct Assistant Professor of Architecture at Rice University, and RICENTRO Program Director at the Rice Center for Community Design and Research.

legal parameters, have been seen as blighted areas that must be removed and replaced by institutional means, and later, as homogeneous settlements marginal to the rapid growth of urban areas, but significant in their internal organization, spontaneous creation and development, and potential impact on the city's economic and political life. Only recently has the importance of squatter settlements been identified—that of viable, adaptive physical environments which allow their occupants to participate in and benefit from development.

Moreover, the growth and change which takes place in these settlements, transforming aggregations of dwelling units (however rudimentary in nature) into a mature urban community with a full range of public and private services, is duplicated in government-sponsored settlements for similar income groups. This evolution is brought about by investment and construction under the control of the dwellers themselves. Their housing costs are kept as low as possible and real economic gains are made from the provision of housing and commercial services to the settlements' inhabitants, facts which affect income distribution.

The phenomenon as it occurs in Bogotá, Colombia, is influenced by the availability of land, construction materials, and key public services, and by the decision of the settlement dwellers to exercise control over the creation and/or maintenance of their physical environment. All of these are dynamic factors whose modification could bring about reduction or cessation of settlement development.

Section II of the paper deals with squatter settlements and their role as traditionally understood in resolving urban housing and development issues. The dynamics of these settlements are explored to better understand the settlements' participation in the low income housing sector. Section III discusses housing and community, describing how low income settlements, regardless of origin, take part in common development processes. In Section IV, some specific characteristics of low income family settlements and sources of income that are derived from investment in building space are examined. Finally, in Section V, some summary observations are made concerning the future development of these settlements.

II. SQUATTER SETTLEMENTS IN AN URBAN GROWTH AND CHANGE CONTEXT

Squatter settlements have been the dominant force in shaping the large urbanized areas in Latin America. Their formation and growth have brought into focus the problems of rapid in-migration of peasants from rural and semi-rural areas. Housing becomes the immediate and most pressing need of these migrants, a need which they are both able and accustomed to provide for themselves.

The formation of such settlements on the edges of urban areas has traditionally been seen in varying ways. These views have developed out of the realization by governments, planners, and academicians that tremendous growth was taking place in urban areas after the Second World War. The post-war era produced a development boom in most Latin American countries. Urban places expanded as the countries began to industrialize. Rising urban incomes brought about a rapid in-migration to urban areas—ports, industrialized agricultural and mineral extraction centers—of rural peasants seeking employment, education, health care, and the other services urbanized areas could offer. Colonial towns became cities and colonial cities grew rapidly, their character changing from a meeting place between a primarily agricultural-based society and its produce exchange for imported consumer goods, to one of a center for the production and consumption of goods.

The inner core of the expanding urban areas had been developed during colonial times as residential centers by and for those who controlled both the agricultural production and the commercial arenas. Imported advances in transportation and communication, and massive public works projects now allowed those inhabitants to establish residential enclaves on the perimeter of the urban areas, leaving the colonial cores as their business centers. The vacated colonial dwellings were quickly converted into dense low cost rental units and were rapidly occupied by the peasant influx.

This housing stock being consumed, the migrants were then forced to seek housing solutions through other means. Housing institutions, both the private and the newly established public agencies that supplied dwelling units to the middle and upper economic classes, did not respond adequately to the needs of the lower economic class. Alternatives had to be sought outside the existing social, legal, and physical order, generally taking the form of provisional shelters, rudimentary in nature, illegally built on publicly or privately held land in a clandestine manner by migrant families acting individually or in large groups, often numbering in the thousands. Land could also be attained from private entrepreneurs who, capable of withstanding social and political pressure, would sell parcels illegally.[3] These areas grew quickly as cities doubled in size every twenty years, with low income families approaching 50% of the urban population.

Seen on the one hand, the growth of *invasion* and "illegal" housing settlements was condoned, perhaps even secretly supported, by governmental agencies and political parties if only to gain the political support of the migrants, silence their demand for housing, and avert facing the major problems of urban development directly.[4] This was accompanied by official political and professional positions declaring such settlements as festering sores—rings of poverty, filth, and political radicalism that encircled and threatened the peaceful and orderly social, economic, and physical operation of cities. Settlements were decried as illegal, unplanned, dangerous growths that blighted the environment and whose only solution was eradication.[5] At the same time national and international development interests recognized the potential promise and danger of a rapidly urbanizing Latin America and sought to create standards and master plans to guide and control growth and development.[6]

During the 1960s, the study of the origins and organizations of these settlements began. It became apparent that while their development was outside the framework of traditional, overt powers and controls, the settlements had mass political potential and (in and among themselves) possessed a high degree of planning and organization. The view of squatter settlements changed to one of marginality—a group of homogeneous developments characterized by illegal land tenure and owner-built housing, with a migrant base, but necessarily outside the mainstream of urban life. Studies emphasized the internal organization of the settlements and their roles in the urbanization of peasants as the last step of the rural to urban, colonial core to fringe settlement migration pattern.[7] It was recognized that the settlement dweller's objective in coming to the city to seek opportunities was fulfilled to the greatest extent through acquisition of housing. The social and physical redeeming graces of squatter settlements and their part in providing housing were explained.

The "festering sore" view of squatter settlement development demanded overt control of urban growth by traditional means, assuming that settlements could be forcefully removed and replaced by institutionalized housing solutions. The "marginality" view suggested that the settlement phenomenon was separate from its larger urban context, particularly physically, and established a characterization of homogeneous micro-organizations residual to urban growth as a whole. Neither view is adequate.

Squatter settlements are diverse in their characteristics. Their formation takes place in a variety of patterns that respond to social and political organization, leadership availability, economic status, and ability to operate effectively in the larger urban environment. Migration may take place directly to the settlement from rural or semi-rural areas without participation in the inner city urbanization process.[8] Although their adult population is still predominantly migrant, squatter settlement population will soon be composed largely of first generation urban dwellers.

Land tenure is more complex than was originally presumed. Invasions and illegal formation of settlements form the basic land acquisition methods, later complemented by organized, complex systems of buying, selling, and renting land parcels. The development potential of squatter settlements, which give an opportunity for capital formation through land acquisition and building, not only has been recognized by the dwellers themselves, but also has been discovered by the more traditional and institutional land development interests, who have sought entrance into the market.[9]

Self-help housing (*autoconstruccion*), the term usually applied to owner-built dwelling units, has generally characterized the housing development, but there is a growing occurrence of owner-contracted housing, built by a variety of subcontractors for fees or in-kind services by the owner. The volume of such construction approaches conventional housing construction in quantity and represents a substantial part of total consumption of construction materials.[10]

Most importantly, squatter settlements have shaped the urban areas. Their development responds to locational factors in much the same fashion as other sectors of the private housing market. Because of their magnitude, they have dramatically altered the growth patterns of many cities, forming away from and beyond the existing infrastructure of the city, thus dictating where future transportation and other services must be located. Substantially altering master plans, their growth demands a review of existing construction standards, zoning and building ordinances, and housing policies and programs. Squatter settlements are the most dynamic, adaptive physical environment in the urban setting, reflecting a determination and ability to grow and change.[11]

III. HOUSING: SHELTER AND COMMUNITY

Much of the study of squatter settlements stems from the view that these communities have one function to perform—that of shelter. Their formation and development are seen as evolving from fulfillment of this need.

Squatter settlements certainly have as their basis the provision of shelter. Because of the inability of settlement dwellers to gain substantial control over the provision for other needs they possess—employment, education, health services, transportation, clothing, food—they find shelter the only necessity of their daily lives over which they can exact overt control. Whether inside or outside the existing social, economic, and political standards, shelter is obtained.

Governments and institutions, in the face of rapidly increasing urban population, seek to provide housing alternatives for low income families. The objective is to house as many families as economically and efficiently as possible. Minimum space standards become maximum accommodations. The production of dwelling units (shelter) through a variety of projects—self help, sweat equity (investment in housing through manual labor), sites and services, core units, etc.—often becomes the short, medium, and long-range goals of the housing programs.

At the outset, then, squatter settlements and public sector housing begin at the same level: shelter. And just as shelter reflects only one need, aggregations of housing units at their inception represent only the static beginning to a dynamic process of creating a community. Growth and change occurs. Communities mature; commercial uses are immediately introduced; infrastructure elements are upgraded or established if not already present. A transformation takes place which allows for integration into the larger urban context.

The growth and change which takes place in the settlements provides for security of ownership, protection from the elements, investment in housing as formation of capital, supplementing family income with home-based business, and the need to establish and identify the dwelling as a personal possession.[12]

For Bogotá, it would appear that the issue should not be the share of production of low income housing the public and private sectors must assume, but whether these sectors will be able to continue to deliver the opportunity for evolutionary development of housing at the same rate that it has been delivered in the past. *Autoconstruccion* (self-built housing through private sector initiative and government housing programs) has accounted for approximately 50% of the housing unit starts in Bogotá in recent years.[13] These settlements have been instrumental in providing shelter to low income families, as well as opportunities for formation of capital, immediate utilization of available disposable income, reduction of housing costs, and sources of income through renting or creation of non-residential uses.

There are advantages, however, to the government's taking a more dominant role in the development of urban areas, particularly with regard to the development of low income housing. Because of the explosion of squatter settlement development over the last three decades, the ability of the government in most cases to determine growth patterns has been minimal. The principal advantages of planning for further growth, however, do not lie so much in the more efficient development of the dwelling unit itself,[14] as in the guiding of the growth of the city as a whole and, most importantly, in the adequate provision of necessary transportation, utilities, health, education, and social services.

IV. INCOME AND LOW INCOME HOUSING DEVELOPMENT

Because the preponderance of low income families find housing solutions through self-contracted, self-help means in the *invasion, pirata,* and government sectors of the housing market, it is necessary to examine the income characteristics of those families and the importance the dwelling unit as a source of income. DANE estimates that 50% of all Bogotá households earn less than 2,500 pesos (1970) per month.[15] Family income categories are distributed across the housing submarket groups as shown in table 1.

TABLE I
FAMILY INCOME BY HOUSING SUBMARKETS, BOGOTÁ

Income/month (1970 pesos)	*Invasion*	*Pirata*	Government	Commercial	Total units	Percentage
0-500	653	9,392	1,930	21,530	33,505	7.4
501-1250	2,863	87,897	8,673	21,850	121,283	26.9
1251-2500	1,333	85,143	21,419	13,431	121,326	26.9
2501-4000	104	21,847	10,295	61,382	93,628	20.8
4001+	—	—	6,426	74,934	91,360	18.0
Total	4,955	204,182	48,740	193,124	451,102	100.0
Percentage	1.1	45.3	10.8	42.8	100.0	

Source: Valenzuela and Vernez, *La Actividad Constructora Popular: Analisis General Y Elementos Para Una Politica de Apoyo* (DNP, April 1972), p. 27.

Since the dwelling units these families occupy are primarily single family attached units built over an extended period (excluding the commercial submarket), it can be assumed that 79.4% (from tables 1 and 2) of families with monthly incomes of 2,500 pesos or less are finding their housing solution as owners, renters, or roomers in self-contracted units.[16] Examining the housing tenure status of these families brings into focus the importance of accumulation of capital through the housing development process. In tenure status, owners represent the majority in all housing submarkets except the commercial (see table 2).[17] Renters occupy the majority of commercial submarket units and approximately one-fifth of the *pirata* units, but are not found in the government submarket (government housing for this income category offers ownership rather than rental programs). For the *pirata* and government submarkets, roomers account for a significant portion of the households and most likely represent the portion above unity (.2 to .3) of the ratio of the number of households per dwelling unit (1.2 to 1.3).[18]

TABLE 2
HOUSEHOLD DISTRIBUTION BY HOUSING SUBMARKET AND HOUSING TENURE

Housing submarket	Tenure owners	Renters	Roomers	Total percentage
Pirata	52.9	19.7	27.4	100.0
Invasion	61.8	0.0	38.2	100.0
Government	85.7	0.0	14.3	100.0
Commercial	34.7	65.3	—	100.0

Source: Valenzuela and Vernez, *Actividad Constructora Popular: Analisis General Y Elementos Para Una Politica de Apoyo* (DNP, April 1972), p. 30.

Berry's previous studies of housing expenditures indicate that for the *pirata* settlements, 51% of the households pay nothing for housing services,[19] a figure approximately equal to the 52.9% of the households who are owners in this housing submarket. In *invasion* settlements, an even higher percentage pays nothing for housing services.

For those households in this low income category (2,500 pesos or less per month) that do pay for housing services, the cost is generally 20-25% of monthly incomes.[20] Actual payments seldom exceed 500 pesos and are seldom less than 150 pesos[21] with a median cost of 200 to 250 pesos.[22]

If the fraction of households per dwelling unit over unity (.2 to .3) can be attributed to roomers in owner occupied or rented dwelling units, it can be estimated that for the families who rent to roomers (approximately 25%), the income derived is 26% of total monetary income (median rent paid divided by median total income).[23] This figure, no doubt, varies greatly from household to household.

A study limited to three distinct settlements—*invasion, pirata,* and government—at different levels of development and distinct locations in the city, indicates a similar occurrence of roomers and income generated. The percentage of dwelling units with roomers varies between 38% and 22% for the government and *pirata* settlements, respectively (both settlements more than 85% developed into permanent structures).[24] The percentage of total monthly income represented by income from dwelling units with roomers is 24.1% for the government settlement and 21.5% for the *pirata*.[25] The study indicates that the roomers occupied 1.6 rooms per dwelling or 27.2% of the total rooms in the unit (excluding baths, patios, and storage areas). Although more detailed study of the phenomenon is necessary, these figures may serve to indicate the importance of renting as an income source to a primary occupant of a dwelling unit who has the ability to develop and expand his unit to other uses over a period of time.

Current migration patterns reinforce the importance of offering housing services to low income migrant families. Vernez estimates that between 50% and 80% of the immigrants to arrive in Bogotá became roomers in *pirata* and *invasion* settlements. Only 7% to 27% of the immigrants arriving go first to the city's center, their traditional destination,[26] the remaining migrants going directly to low income settlement areas. Migrants pay a portion of their income as rent to families who are investing that income in developing housing services. Self-contracted housing, then, includes self-financing. Low income families provide housing solutions for families with income characteristics similar to theirs, substantially aiding in the resolution of the housing shortage in Bogotá, and, at the same time, increase their ownership of capital.

A second important source of revenue for low income families is utilization of the dwelling unit for nonresidential purposes. There has been little study done of the importance of non-wage income as part of the total earnings of low income families. Given that underemployment or occasional employment is prevalent among low income families, the opportunities to supplement fixed income with rental of dwelling unit space for non-residential uses or the use of space by the family for business or commercial concerns deserves attention. Berry states that when small shops in the dwelling provide the principal income source for the family, incomes from these businesses surpass wages from labor or salaried employment. Moreover, a small sample study in Bogotá and Cali indicates that goods-producing shops represent the principal income for 14-25% of the families.[27]

A land use inventory of the three previously mentioned settlements plus an additional *pirata* and *invasion* settlement (both more than 75% developed into permanent construction), done by the author in 1973, shows that 21-29% of all dwelling units quarter some type of non-residential use.[28] The percentage of different types of non-residential use is shown in table 3.

TABLE 3

NONRESIDENTIAL USES IN FIVE LOW INCOME SETTLEMENTS (BOGOTÁ)

Settlement	Small food store	Small production shop (goods)	Small retail shop (goods & services)	Restaurant	Office	Percentage
Pirata	30.3	21.4	22.3	16.5	9.5	100.0
Invasion	38.0	27.5	19.7	11.3	3.5	100.0
Government	25.2	18.9	30.8	9.4	15.7	100.0

Source: Bender Settlement Land Use Inventory, 1973-74.

The most prevalent activities found are those which provide commercial goods and services to the community (small food stores, small retail shops, and restaurants). These are probably operated by someone other than the head of the household—the women and children in the family—who can operate the businesses while carrying on the functions of the family. The two remaining activities (small production shops and offices) most likely are activities carried on by the heads of households, and they perhaps offer employment to other persons.[29] Although no detailed information concerning income from these activities is available, the study by Bender and Gauhan may provide some insight. For the first group of activities—conducted by non-heads of households—the incomes from these represented 15.9, 21.7, and 25.5% of total income in *pirata, invasion,* and government settlements, respectively. For those activities conducted by heads of households, the percentages were 19.5, 24.9, and 13.4%, respectively. The lower percentage in the government settlement for the second group is probably due to the income requirements of the government housing programs, which tend to accept heads of households with stable employment. In addition, the reduced size of rooms and lots in the government programs make space allocations to nonresidential uses difficult.

Of the nonresidential uses identified in the three-settlement study, less than 13% occur in rooms identified as rented space, indicating that these activities are carried on by the primary occupants of the dwelling unit. Comparing the percentage of total income that these business activities represent and the rental value of the space they occupy, it appears that the return is approximately the same. Moreover, as Berry points out, these shops often provide the family with goods at wholesale prices, thus increasing the value of having a business in the dwelling unit.[30] There would also appear to be more family satisfaction in operating a business, in that it gives the appearance (if not the income) that the family is progressing and economically active. Also, business activities may interfere less with family life than the presence of roomers who must share sanitary facilities.

Less than 2% of those dwelling units with roomers indicated that they also rented space for nonresidential uses. Unfortunately, specific data is not available as to whether or not roomers are also present in those dwelling units with businesses operated by dwelling owners or renter families. From the above, it would seem that it is improbable. Since dwellings in these settlements tend to have 5.77 rooms and 7 persons per unit, it can be assumed that no more than 1 to 1.6 rooms per dwelling would be devoted to nonfamily use (the family occupying a living area, kitchen, and two sleeping areas).

Summing the percentages of dwelling units with nonresidential uses and those with roomers, 10% to 57% of the dwelling units surveyed utilize dwelling unit space as an income producing source representing 15% to 25% of the total monthly family income. While further study is needed in this area, the Bender-Gauhan study indicates the importance of the dwelling unit as an income source to the families during the development of the settlement.

TABLE 4

SPACE UTILIZATION IN LOW INCOME SETTLEMENTS (BOGOTÁ)

	Settlement		
	Pirata	*Invasion**	Government
% Nonresidential	21	7	19
% Boarders	22	3	38
% Total	43	10	57

*The low percentage of income producing uses in the *invasion* settlement is due to its state of development and location rather than to its condition of being an *invasion* settlement (see note 30).

Sources: Bender Land Use Survey in Five Bogotá Settlements, 1973-74; Bender and Gauhan Settlement Study, 1973-74.

Almost all income producing use of dwelling unit space takes place in units which are of permanent construction. Rental of space to roomers is most commonly found in smaller units and is associated with households with lower incomes. Nonresidential activities are likewise most generally found in dwelling units of permanent construction, and total monthly incomes of the households who own the units are usually higher than incomes of those who rent space.

In summary, the income derived from utilization of dwelling unit space can be matched with perceived opportunities for investment by the dwelling unit owner. Needs can be closely matched to resources at any given moment, providing a flexibility that is not offered by other investment opportunities. It is doubtful that the available funds and labor of low income families can be invested in other sectors so effectively and efficiently.

A third important source of income to the settlement families is the housing expenditure relief that possession of dwelling unit (with or without legal title) represents. As noted earlier, it is estimated that half of the low income families in the *pirata* settlements pay nothing for housing services.

The amount that this housing expenditure relief represents as a percentage of total income calls for comment. Since most units average from 4.5 (*invasion*) to 6.6 (*pirata*) rooms per dwelling,[31] it can be assumed that for dwelling units without rental space the value of monthly housing services consumed is from 1,125 to 1,650 pesos (250 pesos per room) for units without rental space, and from 750 to 1,125 pesos for units with rented space.[32] Table 5 presents the imputed value of housing services as a percentage of total monthly family income.

TABLE 5
IMPUTED VALUE OF HOUSING SERVICES
(Percentage of Total Monthly Family Income*)

Settlement		Monetary Family Income Level (pesos)		
		1,250	2,500	4,000
Pirata unit	w/rental space	47.4%	31.0%	22.0%
	w/o rental space	61.1%	39.8%	29.2%
Invasion unit	w/rental space	37.5%	23.1%	15.6%
	w/o rental space	47.4%	31.0%	22.0%

*Based on 1) 4.5 rooms/dwelling unit in *invasion* settlements and 6.5 rooms/dwelling unit in *pirata* settlements, 2) 250 pesos per room per month rent, and 3) 1.5 rooms rented.

Although only approximate in nature, the percentage of total income represented by the consumption of housing services is significant, particularly in the lower income categories. Clearly, if families who possess dwelling units in these settlements were forced to seek housing on the rental market, it would be extremely difficult for them to duplicate the services that they are now consuming. They, like the families to whom they rent, would be forced to locate in fewer rooms, lose the income resources the dwelling unit represents, and pay a significant portion of their real income for rent.

V. SOME SUMMARY REMARKS

The income generated through rents and home-based businesses, and the reduction of housing costs through home ownership, are significant when compared with the total incomes for low income families. The opportunity for these families to continue to better their economic situation through this type of housing development is changed, however, by several key issues. Access to land, availability of construction materials, provision of public services, and the decision to create, develop and maintain one's own dwelling are priority issues to be dealt with if the process is to continue.

The issue of access to land is critical. Clearly, land costs will be an important factor in determining the composition of the housing market in Bogotá in the future, the locational characteristics low income family settlements will have, and the type and density of dwelling units that will be developed. Undeveloped land will have to be made available to low income families at affordable prices. Although little empirical information is available at present, it appears important to understand the trade-offs between long-range development of dwelling units which may be modified over a period of time and short-range development of multifamily, multistory structures, which support high land costs, but which may be modified to an extremely limited degree. Given the importance of income generated from dwelling unit use, it would seem unlikely that the multifamily, multistory solution is appropriate unless the opportunity cost of using the dwelling unit as an income source is replaced by higher, fixed-wage incomes or by a subsidy. If ownership of capital (land and its improvements) is now seen as the most effective way of redistributing income while achieving growth, housing may prove to be the most accessible capital to be acquired by the poor.

Regarding provision of public services, low income housing settlements are often established before there is adequate provision of water and sewerage systems, paved streets, public transportation, education and health facilities, telephones, etc. This is particularly true in the case of *invasion* and *pirata* settlements. A long process through legal, political, and administrative channels then ensues to bring these services to the community, unless the settlements themselves attempt to provide them. Major development loan commitments of international and national agencies for provision of such services reflects the high priority given them by local governments and dwellers, although few studies have been conducted examining settlement origin, development patterns, and the impact these services have on the ability of the settlements to develop. Given the limited amount of resources available for utility provision, priorities must be established which will enhance development capabilities. It is clear, however, that continued growth and development of low income housing settlements is dependent on their inclusion into the urban network of services.

The issue of availability of construction materials is similar to that of land accessibility. Limited quantities of basic construction materials are available. Settlement dwellers must purchase these materials on the open market, competing with the demands created by the institutionalized housing industry and the transportation, commercial, and manufacturing sectors. Unavailability of construction materials because of price or production severely limits the ability of the settlements to grow and expand, thus reducing the amount of housing and commercial services offered through settlement development.

Housing policies that increase the production of middle and upper income housing would appear to have as one effect a reduction of construction activity in low income family settlements, through decreasing the limited supply and inflating the cost of construction materials. Wages earned in the production of higher income housing by the small segment of the labor force involved in the construction industry may not be directly invested in development of low income housing units. Moreover, given that 45% of all households in Bogotá develop housing in an evolutionary manner, the income gains made by those few in the construction industry may not offset the constraints placed on construction material availability to the majority of the low income families in the city. As in the case of land, the access to construction materials at costs which allow low income families to invest in construction on a continuing basis is essential.

In summary, access to land and construction materials at affordable prices, and provision of public services, are necessary to permit continuing low income settlement development. These issues are, by and large, controlled by forces external to the settlements themselves. The benefits derived from the growth and change that take place enable many of the settlements' inhabitants to survive and prosper in the city.

It is important to remember, however, that a clear decision is made on the part of the low income settlement dweller to assume direct responsibility for the creation and maintenance of his dwelling unit as part of a settlement development process. He not only provides shelter for his family, but also maximizes the opportunity offered by investment in land and improvements made with the income gained through provision of housing and other goods and services.

At present, his decision comes from a lack of alternatives. There is no assurance, however, that future generations will accept direct participation in housing development. Instead, they may demand more traditional alternatives, realizable or not. There is also no guarantee that housing policies and programs will provide the resources necessary for continued settlement development by the dwellers themselves. It cannot be simply assumed that settlement development will continue.

NOTES

I am indebted to CEDE at the Universidad de los Andes and to Edgar Reveiz for their assistance while doing research for the paper in Bogotá. I am grateful to R. Albert Berry and Ronald Soligo for their encouragement and suggestions during the development of the paper. Responsibility for its contents and any errors of conception or fact remain my own.

1. Patrick Geddes, *Town Planning Towards City Development,* a report prepared for the Durbar of Indore, India (1918), I, p. 85.

2. [Sic.] John C. Turner, "A New View of the Housing Deficit," San Juan Seminar Paper (April 1966).

3. This form of development, called *piratas* in Colombia, is especially prevalent in that country, accounting for 41% of all dwelling units in Bogotá; *invasion* settlement dwellings account for only one percent of the total dwelling units. See Jaime Valenzuela and George Vernez, *Actividad Constructora Popular: Analisis General y Elementos Para Una Politica de Apoyo* (DNP, April 1972), p. 68.

4. See David Collier, "The Politics of Squatter Settlement Formation in Peru," February 1973 (mimeograph).

5. See William Mangin, "Latin American Squatter Settlements: A Problem and a Solution," *Latin American Research Review* **1**, no. 3 (Summer 1967): 65-98.

6. This parallels policy and planning thinking in most western, industrialized nations, particularly in the United States, laying the groundwork for vast urban renewal projects in deteriorated urban areas, and massive public expenditures to house the urban poor.

7. John C. Turner, "Housing Priorities, Settlement Patterns, and Urban Development in Modernizing Countries," *American Institute of Planners Journal* **34**, no. 6 (November 1968): 354-363.

8. Albert Berry, *Algunas Caracteristicas del Sector de Auto Construccion de Viviendas: Proyecciones de Su Importancia Relativa El Futuro* (DNP, 1972), p. 16; hereafter cited as Berry.

9. Research is underway to examine the legal aspects of *pirata* land sales and settlement development in Bogotá (FEDESARROLLO).

10. Valenzuela and Vernez, *Actividad Constructora Popular,* p. 13.

11. See DESAL, *Marginalidad en America Latina,* I and II (Santiago, Chile, 1967). For a critical analysis of this concept, see Jose Nun, "La Marginalidad en America Latina," *Revista Latinoamerica de Sociologia* **2** (July 1969).

12. Turner, "Housing Priorities," pp. 354-363.

13. Berry, p. 7.

14. It seems doubtful that more controlled construction practices in the development of low income housing, although eliminating some of the inefficiency incurred through phased construction, can offset hidden costs in administration, under-utilization of resources (time, money, exchange of services, etc.), and general loss of control of the owner over the building process.

15. DANE, Encuesta de Hogares (E-H2) (unpublished tables); see DAPD, *Mercadeo de Tierras en Barrios Clandestinos de Bogotá* (April 1973), p. 10.

16. Roomers include the "inquilinatos" or those who rent rooms from a household, sharing common sanitary facilities. As will be discussed later, the government housing solutions offered in this income category are of a self-contracted nature, with the family making modifications and/or additions to the units they build or buy through the government programs. See Valenzuela and Vernez, *Actividad Constructora Popular,* pp. 27 and 30.

17. *Invasion* settlements are eliminated from the discussion because of their minor role (1.8% of total families) in housing this income category (see table 1).

Renters and roomers represent 65.3% of the families in the commercial submarket. Moreover, this submarket houses the poorest segment of the population—76.0% of the families in the submarket have household incomes of 1,250 pesos or less.

18. See DAPD, *Mercadeo de Tierras,* p. 78.

19. Berry, p. 8.

20. DAPD, *Mercadeo de Tierras,* p. 25.

21. ICT, Normas Minimas.

22. DAPD, *Mercadeo de Tierras,* p. 48.

23. Berry, p. 12.

24. 1974 study of three settlements by Stephen Bender and Timothy Gauhan, Program of Development Studies, Rice University, Houston, Texas.

25. The *invasion* settlement was less than 30% developed into permanent housing, was situated 350 meters above the city in the hills to the southeast of the central business district, and was a 35-minute bus ride away.

26. Berry, p. 16.

27. Ibid., p. 5.

28. The *invasion* settlement mentioned earlier (see note 25) showed only 7% of the dwelling units having some type of nonresidential use. This would appear to be due to the recent establishment of the settlement (1967), the still-provisional condition of most of the construction present, the small size of the dwellings, the noncontiguous, hilly characteristics of the terrain, and the lack of clearly defined streets.

29. Berry, p. 5.

30. Ibid.

31. Bender and Gauhan *Survey.* These figures correspond to 31 m^2 (*invasion*) and 58 m^2 (*pirata*) as described by Valenzuela and Vernez, *Actividad Constructora Popular,* p. 78.

32. Bender and Gauhan Settlement Study, 1973, 1974. Also see DAPD, *Mercadeo de Tierras,* p. 67.

SMALL-SCALE AND TRADITIONAL INDUSTRIES: A DEVELOPMENT ALTERNATIVE

by Yhi-Min Ho and Donald L. Huddle

I. INTRODUCTION

The place of small-scale and traditional industries in the development of less developed countries (LDCs) has received very little attention in the literature or in government development programs.[1] In this paper we intend to consider a development alternative in which the potential role of the sector of small-scale and traditional industries, particularly culturally oriented ones, is explicitly recognized. Because of the particular attributes of this class of industries, we believe they can contribute importantly to the development of LDCs by reducing the degree of inequality in the distribution of gains from development, balancing the geographical distribution of population, and generating employment and foreign exchange earnings. For brevity, we shall call this group of industries the small-scale sector. The study contains four parts. We first examine what we consider the biases and deficiencies of government policies and theoretical models of development that overlook the actual and potential contributions of the small-scale sector. In the second part we discuss the attributes of the small-scale sector and the growth implications of an alternative that incorporates the small-scale sector. In the two remaining sections, we demonstrate the empirical relevancy of our theoretical consideration and consider the type of programs required to develop the sector as a viable source of growth and employment.

II. DEVELOPMENT BIASES AND THEIR CONSEQUENCES

The alternative model of development proposed in this paper is built on the assumption that every development policy has its particular distributional consequences. Thus the common social and economic problems of urban high unemployment and congestion, rural poverty, and the glaring income gaps between the rich and the poor found in most contemporary LDCs reflect the biases and deficiencies in the developmental programs and policies adopted in the past. The terms biases and deficiencies are used in the sense

Mr. Ho is Professor of Economics at the University of St. Thomas. Mr. Huddle is Professor of Economics at Rice University.

that these programs and policies tend either to heighten or to perpetuate the existing degree of inequality in the distribution of gains from development.

From the point of view of equity, the major shortcomings of the present development programs and policies may be specified as 1) too much concern about growth *per se* without due consideration of equity, and 2) too much emphasis on large-scale, capital-intensive techniques and industries. It is also typical of theoretical models of development to describe the essence of development as a process of substitution—capital for labor, industry for agriculture, and modern manufacturing for traditional small-scale industries. Indeed, the substance of development is often seen as the progress from small-scale and traditional industries to modern large-scale industries. Even the coexistence of small-scale, labor-intensive cottage industries in the rural sector with large-scale, capital-intensive industries is generally regarded as a symptom of backwardness in a dualistic economy.

In the classical two-sector growth model,[2] the non-industrial sector is assumed capable of producing only goods for which consumer demand does not grow as rapidly as does income. Therefore, in a growing economy the sector is bound to decline in relative importance in output and employment. The central feature of economic development as theorized in the model is the labor reallocation process from agriculture to industry under fixed real wages. Once growth starts, the industrial sector is assumed to expand smoothly through investment and capital accumulation in the sector. Concurrently, surplus labor is continuously pulled away from agriculture and relocated in industry. Only when the surplus labor in agriculture is totally absorbed by industrial expansion is growth assumed to take on different characteristics. Once growth reaches this important turning point, real wages begin to move upward and the industrial sector tends to assume a capital-intensifying character.

In reality, however, the growth experience in most LDCs in the well-publicized growth decade of the 1960s contradicts the profile described above. There is evidence that a preference for capital-intensive techniques and industries is rather common in the LDCs regardless of their stage of development.[3] Even in countries where the industrial sector has expanded rapidly, the labor reallocation process it generates has never been sizable enough to absorb fully the growth in labor force and the migrated labor from agriculture. The low labor absorption character of industrial expansion is largely attributable to a pattern of development biased toward capital-intensive techniques and industries.

Emphasis on interindustrial linkages and on positive external effects in development programs and projects often leads to a sharp imbalance and high concentration in the geographical distribution of economic activities, hence in the distribution of gains from development.[4] Such a geographic imbalance necessarily encourages the flow of population from rural hinterlands to urban industrial centers in search of employment opportunities that do not exist for the unskilled, unsophisticated peasant migrants. The migrated population that is left unabsorbed by non-agricultural employment inevitably raises social tensions and necessitates a diversion of resources to them for urban services. It is regrettable that in the drive for modernization and industrialization through capital-intensive, large-scale development programs the LDCs are besieged with new social problems of multiple dimensions.

Development strategy that solely emphasizes the development of capital-intensive techniques and industries and large-scale manufacturing may affect the character of the growth process in still another manner. It is generally known that unequal distribution of income is largely due to the unequal distribution of wealth. Given the distribution of wealth, the impact of its inequality may be lessened if the share of income from property in national income decreases and the share of labor correspondingly increases. The share of labor in national income is least likely to rise in an economy in which demand for capital increases relative to labor because of the capital-biased character of development policies.

It is therefore not surprising to find that in the theoretical framework of the two-sector growth models for the LDCs, little attention is given to the small-scale sector as a means of promoting development and as a means of lessening the social and economic frictions that growth brings. Activities and industries in the small-scale sector are invariably characterized as backward and inefficient.[5] The products of the sector are also considered inferior in quality to those produced by large-scale methods. The consumer is assumed to favor the latter. Thus, as development proceeds and income rises, firms and industries in the sector are assumed to be replaced by modern large-scale manufacturing.

III. AN ALTERNATIVE MODEL OF DEVELOPMENT INCORPORATING THE SMALL-SCALE SECTOR

We present here an alternative model that is a direct challenge to the one prescribed in the two-sector development models for the LDCs. If consideration is given to the distribution aspect of development programs and policies, in our view the core of the development solution in the LDCs should be the creation of substantially more productive employment in modern industries or, if not here, elsewhere. Admittedly, development and growth imply changes in the employment structure. And structural change often means the relative decline in importance of rural based, agriculture-related economic activities. Although a decline in these industries has actually been observed, the phenomenon should not be generalized as an investment criterion for development. Measured changes in the employment structure may merely be a statistical fallacy if a growing part of the working age population is left either underemployed or unemployed.

Moreover, we question the validity of the generalization that products of the small-scale sector are necessarily inferior and that the sector should necessarily decline because of low income elasticities for its products in a growing economy. We find it useful for analytical as well as policy purposes to divide the small-scale, traditional industries sector into two distinctly different groups. For identification purposes we shall call them Type I and Type II.

We define Type I as the segment of the small-scale sector that produces non-traditional, manufactured products. These manufactured products may be produced more efficiently by larger-scale firms. Type I firms are thus definitely technically inferior to larger firms because of their small scale of operations. The existence of such firms and activities can be explained only in terms of market imperfection and constraints on market size. Therefore, their presence is pertinent only to a particular stage of development. Given time, firms or industries in the group will either grow in size through development or will disappear through competition. Current examples from Asia include bicycle production, decorative lights, and some textiles and clothing.

Type II industries are firms that specialize in hand-made goods, artistic products, and other products with a distinctive cultural character. The product distinction of these goods is directly derived from the small-scale, labor-intensive process of production. Thus the small scale of operation in this instance is a definite market advantage rather than a disadvantage. More importantly, we believe that the products are highly demanded as consumers' incomes rise. Hand-made woolen and cotton clothing, and leather goods, are the best examples of such products; jewelry, pottery, straw products, ceramics, and local Indian crafts are also excellent examples of what we have in mind.

The theoretical structure of the development alternative proposed here recognizes the existence of a small-scale subsector, capable of producing goods that increase with income, in the traditional rural sector.[6] The model consists of an industrial sector, an agricultural sector, and a small-scale subsector within the agricultural sector; it produces a new set of growth implications significantly different from those drawn from the two-sector growth models.

In our new model, the labor reallocation process from agriculture to industry is no longer necessarily the most important dimension of growth. Growth can take place without labor reallocation. Development and expansion of the small-scale sector can create employment opportunities for labor released by agriculture. Since we believe that firms and activities in the small-scale sector are largely rural based, the magnitude of labor reallocation can be minimized, if not eliminated. The process of modernization as seen from this alternative approach is not merely a substitution of industry for agriculture, of capital-intensive, large-scale manufacturing for labor-intensive, small-scale, traditional industries. Rather, the model postulates that development and expansion of the small-scale sector may provide a source of growth and an impetus toward modernization for the LDCs. In essence, the alternative model suggests that a wholesome, balanced approach to development requires coordinated efforts in promoting industrial and agricultural development on the one hand, and modern manufacturing and small-scale industries on the other hand.

Our alternative view of development does not deny that historically certain types of traditional industries have been both non-competitive in production and unresponsive in demand when faced with competition from larger scale, more efficient manufacturing production.[7] Such a general characterization of all products and activities within the small-scale sector is not accurate, however. Nor does the model suggest that the small-scale sector entirely replaces the industrial sector in the development process. The model does suggest that the development of the small-scale sector should be integrated into overall development programs to complement industrial and agricultural transformation in the LDCs. Because of the unique features that products and firms in the small-scale sector possess, development of the sector may make significant contributions in the following areas:

1) Employment creation. As we have argued in section II, development of large-scale, capital-intensive techniques and industries has been given priority in the LDCs for over a quarter of a century, but has not provided the desired amount of employment in spite of rapid growth in output. It is of great social importance therefore that a solution be found. We hypothesize on *a priori* grounds that products of the small-scale sector have higher employment content than most large-scale manufacturing activities. It follows that a given amount of investment in the small-scale sector will create more employment than it would create in manufacturing. It is true that the small-scale sector normally has relatively low value added per worker, implying relatively low wage rates. But low wage rates do not seem too important in economies where labor has few alternative skills or opportunities.

Since the small-scale sector could put to work a part of the rural population that might otherwise be left out, the gains from development of the small-scale sector are likely to be spread over a broad base and therefore to improve income distribution.

2) Balance in geographic distribution. A conspicuous phenomenon common to the contemporary LDCs is an unevenness in the geographical distribution of economic activities and a resulting regional inequality in income distribution. The regional inequality and geographical imbalance inevitably set the labor migration process in motion, from the retarded to the growing regions. Population movement is both socially necessary and desirable as long as the migrated labor force is subsequently absorbed into productive employment. Evidence has shown, however, that the labor absorption rate of industrial expansion has typically been low in the LDCs relative to the magnitude of migration and growth in the labor force, implying that regional imbalance and high urban unemployment and congestion are closely related. In addition, migration of the labor force is known to be selective; it is mostly concentrated in the youngest and best educated. As a result, the quality of the remaining labor force in the migrating sector deteriorates. Regional imbalance is thus partly responsible for rural poverty and stagnation. Possibly a diversified geographical and industrial structure may provide a better solution to the problems of high urban unemployment and rural development, compared to the alternative of continued centralization and growth of cities with accompanying external factors that decrease amenities of life and increase costs of government and costs of urban living.

Our interest in the development of the small-scale sector lies partly in its tendency to be rural based. Expansion of the sector can slow the destabilizing flow of population to the urban areas insofar as employment opportunity in the rural as well as urban areas is a fundamental variable in the migratory flow equation.

3) Trade and export potential. The present structure of international trade, as viewed in the well-known neoclassical theory of comparative advantage, is characterized by the flow of industrial and manufactured goods from the developed to the developing countries, and the flow of raw materials and agricultural products in the opposite direction. The developing countries in the Third World have been highly critical of this pattern of trade.[8] The existing pattern of international trade is looked upon as a mechanism through which the industrial centers exploit the periphery. Although the recent oil crisis and other raw material shortages may have temporarily turned the argument around, the fact remains that developing countries rich in resources are the fortunate few. Most LDCs still must accept the existing pattern of international trade. Moreover, in the foreseeable future, it is highly unlikely that the present directions of trade will reverse. If one looks ahead realistically, export expansion in light manufactured goods and goods that are produced by labor-intensive and small-scale industries, particularly those with a distinctive cultural character, provides a promising avenue for growth.

IV. THE EMPIRICAL RELEVANCE OF THE MODEL

The theoretical validity and empirical relevance of the alternative model of development undoubtedly depend on the question of whether a set of products and activities having the special attributes we describe exists in the rural sector of contemporary LDCs. To test this proposition, we identified some eighty-one SITC (Standard International Trade Classification) commodities that met the following two criteria: 1) they are produced or producible by small-scale, traditional industries, and 2) they are either presently traded or potentially tradable on the international market.[9] In the initial phase of testing the empirical relevance of the model, we concentrate on the set of commodities of the small-scale sector traded on the international market because most other published data are not disaggregated enough to allow the type of empirical test the model requires. In addition, the impetus for the development of the small-scale sector in LDCs may initially come from its successful penetration into markets in the developed countries.

Although the SITC categories were less disaggregated and complete than we would have liked, we pieced together three sets of operable data: 1) U.S. import data between 1964 and 1970 annually, 2) a combined cross-section of import data for fifteen OECD countries for 1968 and 1969, and 3) a combined cross-section of import data for fifteen OECD countries for 1968 and 1969, confined strictly to imports from the LDCs. Evidence derived from the econometric study of the data indicates that: 1) Import demand for the eighty-one selected commodities had high income elasticities (in most instances both individual category and total income elasticity estimates are far above unity[10]); 2) the eighty-one SITC commodities were internationally traded in important quantities from 1964 to 1970, with rates of expansion even exceeding those of general manufacturing (import demand for products with cultural distinction grew at 11.6% per annum on the average versus about 9% per annum for all manufactures); and 3) all items in the set we have investigated were goods of high labor content. Moreover, an analysis based on the cross-section data for the fifteen OECD countries suggests that the higher the labor content, the higher was the income elasticity of import demand.

Explicitly, the results confirm our *a priori* hypothesis that a group of small-scale goods of high income elasticity does exist. Contrary to the assertion that products of the small-scale sector decline in relative importance as income rises, as a group they have expanded as well as, and in many instances better than, all internationally traded goods in a period of rapidly growing trade. In fact, numerous other goods that may be produced by the small-scale sector in the LDCs are yet to be identified. And others currently traded on the international market can increase in importance if concerted efforts are made in financing and marketing.

The rapid expansion of demand for such small-scale, traditional products is not difficult to explain, particularly with respect to their market expansion in the affluent, developed economies. The basic reason is that tastes are changing toward differentiated, distinctive products as the growing middle class in the wealthy nations becomes more affluent. As affluence has become widespread the vast middle income class is responding to the same product attributes (connected to craftsmanship and the local culture) as the ruling (wealthy) class did in the past. Also, as the mass of consumers has become more highly educated, their wants and tastes have become more distinctive. In this setting, mass produced factory goods, particularly consumer goods, lose much of their appeal (though they still dominate the total market), whereas hand-made, non-standardized goods of artistic merit and goods reflecting definitely distinctive cultural character become more appealing. The markets for products from the small-scale sector are likely to grow as development reaches more advanced stages. Though such products might be thought to be greatly subject to fads and fickleness in the market (since they are not necessities), our econometric evidence indicates that they are no more so than industrial products generally.

V. IMPLICATIONS FOR POLICIES AND CONCLUDING REMARKS

Having theorized a development model explicitly incorporating the small-scale sector, and having demonstrated the empirical relevance of the model, we now turn to the discussion of significant policy issues implied by the model.[11]

First, we find it is essential to recognize that the small-scale sector is a heterogeneous aggregation of firms that analytically can be separated into at least two groups. The classification of Type I and Type II industries in our analytical framework is made on the basis of the importance of the scale factor in the determination of operational efficiency and the market characteristics of the products. Whereas the scale of operation is unimportant and products are income elastic for Type II industries, smallness in scale and income inelasticity of products are seen as disadvantages of Type I industries in the small-scale sector.

Conceivably there are similarities and overlappings in the problems and difficulties they face. We see, however, a fundamental difference in the ultimate objective of developmental policies in dealing with the two groups. That is, the relative importance of Type I industries in the sector should be reduced and correspondingly the share of Type II should be expanded if the small-scale sector is to become a more important source of growth. Accordingly, projects and programs designed to develop the sector should fully take into account the scale factor and demand characteristics that separate the firms and industries in the sector.

Empirical findings from field work in the LDCs suggest that further distinctions can be made between economies of scale from production and scale economies derivable from purchasing, marketing, and financing. Often small scale appears to be a market advantage rather than a market disadvantage in production where traditional craftsmanship and skills contribute to the product distinctions. Nevertheless, firms of small size in each subgroup definitely have less access to modern credit facilities and marketing intermediaries. In the area of material purchasing, however, it is possible that both pecuniary and non-pecuniary economies of scale can be made available to some extent to firms in the small-scale sector by the creation of cooperatives and by government interventions in the market. In fact, in order to explore fully the potential of the small-scale sector as a growth agent of significance, we see a need for government efforts and interventions of broader scope, in areas of financing, marketing, and vocational education.

Traditional and small-scale producers must rely almost entirely on self-financing their working and fixed capital requirements. Outside finance is seldom available at competitive rates. In many actual cases in Colombia, Mexico, Hong Kong, and Taiwan small establishments of family workers or of even five to ten hired workers may pay seventy percent interest on a loan, whereas medium and large scale firms will typically borrow at far lower rates of twenty to twenty-five percent. In Taiwan a fairly typical and popular credit arrangement by firms in the sector is to tie credit advances with orders, an arrangement quite similar to the ancient putting-out system. Another popular source of credit for firms in the sector is rural credit cooperatives. Here, larger firms in the sector still benefit more and have more access to funds than the smaller ones. Another deficiency of the rural credit cooperatives as a source of credit is their present limited scope in the rural areas. Nevertheless, rural credit cooperatives appear to be most promising and should be expanded if they can become responsive to needs of small-scale establishments. There are now very few rural or small-scale credit cooperatives in Brazil, Colombia, and Mexico. Most cooperatives exist for purposes of pooling products and marketing.

Of equal importance to finance is the problem of marketing, especially internationally. Few firms in the sector maintain any direct foreign contact. The putting-out system is widely practiced in Taiwan and Hong Kong by the trading firms outside the sector and by larger, newer firms inside the sector, in order to fill large orders from overseas. "Putting-out" characterizes the situation in which the buyer supplies raw materials to the small producer and sets specifications of quality. Private trading firms both produce and purchase from many smaller firms and household producers in Colombia and Mexico. Government cooperatives are of greater importance in these countries and in Brazil as well, while the putting-out system is most important in Hong Kong and Taiwan. But the scope is too limited at the moment to expand the small-scale sector to a size comparable to that defined in our model. Market expansion of products of the small-scale sector to markets in the advanced countries may hold the key to the initial development of the sector in the LDCs. To be successful, governments in the LDCs should undertake efforts in the areas of marketing surveys and quality control to assist firms that have the specified attributes described here in opening up foreign markets. Here again there is some progress in all five countries that we studied, though it often seems to advance at a snail's pace. The trouble in the three Latin American countries is that such efforts are underfinanced and understaffed; also, bureaucratic organizational behavior often leads a life of its own, seemingly even forgetting its original purpose. Good examples abound in all three Latin American cases. In Taiwan and Hong Kong credit cooperatives are very advanced.

The training and education of workers and managers is a problem related to further expansion of the sector and replacement of skilled artisans over a span of years. At present, workers in the sector obtain their training mostly as apprentices in the traditional form, although the governments of the LDCs have also participated in training in varying degrees. It seems that special vocational schools or training centers funded by government might provide a solution to the problem. We also see great potential here in making training available to females of rural households in order to develop supplementary careers for them as producers of handicrafts.

We believe that the needs and problems of the traditional segment of the small-scale sector are qualitatively different from those of the "modernized" handicraft and artistic goods sector. For the "old" section of the small-scale sector, training of workers is closely related to the economic viability of the traditional sector *per se*. That is, needs and problems in marketing, financing, and training should be examined in a consistent manner. One surprising result of our field surveys in Taiwan, Hong Kong, Colombia, Brazil, and Mexico is that in the "new" section of the traditional sector wages and profits are already fairly high—in fact, wages often exceed those of similar workers in large-scale manufacturing. The concern here is that the expansion in production has led to quality deterioration. The problems then are quality control and product design. Neither problem is easily solvable, but it is clear that in the five countries we have studied, artisans have learned in many instances to expand while maintaining quality. The best antidote to quality deterioration is simply rejection of the wares by the marketing agency or purchaser. Product design is a tricky problem, one in which "helpful" governmental nabobs have frequently given artisans bad and costly advice. Still, some hard-won advances are notable in the private and governmental sectors through more trade fairs and various exchanges of information.

Overall, the new, more modern urban handicrafts are faring better than the old, traditional handicrafts from rural zones. The reasons for this are many. In the Latin American cases the rural artisan is less educated, is less willing and able to take risks, and has little if any knowledge of many new possibilities in product design and tastes. Often the producers in the rural zone are the females and even the children. Both produce on a part-time basis when they are not engaged in doing housework or going to school. The husband, with some important exceptions, typically works in agriculture. The artisan's earnings are complementary to the so-called main source of income of the male even though they may be higher than his. To understand the present plight of the rural worker, we need mention only these problems plus exploitation by monopolistic buyers and by middlemen who sell raw materials at prices of up to fifty percent higher than the going rate elsewhere. Governments can, though do not always, behave as exploitatively as the private monopolist and middleman. Probably the best way to overcome the blocks to a potentially efficient and income-raising market opportunity for small producers is for them to organize into larger purchasing and selling units, whether as unions or as cooperatives. In Colombia and Mexico this is precisely what is now happening with some success. In Brazil progress is coming much more slowly, whereas in Hong Kong and Taiwan the "blocks" are less important at this stage of their progress.

We conclude by stating that we share the disillusions brought by the development experience over the past two decades in the LDCs. Our concern for the social and economic problems and our hope for a more equitable distribution of development gains led us to re-examine the place of small-scale and traditional industries in development and international trade and to propose a development alternative contrary to the conventional view of emphasizing growth *per se* and large-scale manufacturing. In our view, the small-scale, traditional industry sector, a sector generally overlooked by policy-makers in the LDCs and by most professional economists, has important contributions to make in lessening some social and economic tensions in the LDCs because of its unique attributes. We find it encouraging that empirical findings have confirmed our *a priori* hypotheses.

In fact, the development of the small-scale sector has taken on a new significance in the midst of the current dislocation of the world economy. The new world economic structure and order that is presently emerging further underlines the importance of such small, labor-intensive industries. One important lesson to be learned from the current economic disorder is that rural development may determine the final outcome of the over-all development efforts in the resource-poor LDCs. Development of the small-scale sector and of agriculture would appear to be two inseparable components of any sustainable rural development strategy.

NOTES

1. In most popular texts on development, neither small-scale industries nor traditional industries are even listed in the indices. See, for example, Benjamin Higgins, *Economic Development* (New York: W. W. Norton, 1968); E. E. Hagen, *The Economics of Development* (Homewood, Ill.: Richard D. Irwin, 1968); H. Bruton, *Principles of Development Economics* (Englewood Cliffs, N.J.: Prentice-Hall, 1965); and J. K. Galbraith, *Economic Development* (Boston: Houghton-Mifflin, Sentry Edition, 1964).

2. The model is elegantly described in W. Arthur Lewis, "Economic Development with Unlimited Supplies of Labor," *Manchester School* **22**, No. 2 (May 1954): 139-191; and John C. H. Fei and Gustav Ranis, *Development of the Labor Surplus Economy* (Homewood, Ill.: Richard D. Irwin, Inc., 1974).

3. Capital-biased growth is found to occur in most Latin American countries; see Werner Baer and M. E. A. Hervé, "Employment and Industrialization in Developing Countries," *Quarterly Journal of Economics* **80**, No. 1 (February 1966): 88-107. The same bias is also found to occur in the Taiwanese development experience in Asia; see Yhi-Min Ho, "Development with Surplus Population—the Case of Taiwan: A Critique of the Classical Two-Sector Model, à la Lewis," *Economic Development and Cultural Change* **20**, No. 2 (January 1972): 210-234.

4. Though A. O. Hirschman was one of the originators and popularizers of the backward and forward linkage approach which has often been used to justify large-scale manufacturing industries as an investment strategy, he himself carefully states that preserving handicrafts and small-scale traditional activities is important. See A. O. Hirschman, *The Strategy of Economic Development* (New Haven: Yale University Press, 1958), p. 131.

5. Cf. Stephen Resnick, "The Decline of Rural Industry under Export Expansion: A Comparison among Burma, Philippines, and Thailand, 1870-1938," *The Journal of Economic History* **30**, No. 1 (March 1970): 51-73; and Stephen Hymer and Stephen Resnick, "A Model of an Agrarian Economy with Nonagricultural Activities," *The American Economic Review* **59**, No. 4 (September 1969): 493-506.

6. Our alternative model of development, by recognizing other non-agricultural activities in the rural sector, is similar to the agrarian model postulated by Hymer and Resnick, "A Model of an Agrarian Economy," but there is a fundamental difference between the two models. That is, non-agricultural activities in the rural sector in their model produce what they call the Z goods, which are assumed to be income-inelastic.

7. Hymer and Resnick, in "A Model of an Agrarian Economy," identify the historical process of replacement of traditional products with the present as well, seeing them as being inferior goods in both domestic and international markets. In fact, Hymer and Resnick appear to have identified all traditional goods as being Z goods when in fact their Z goods pertain to only one portion of the small-scale, traditional goods sector, viz., cottage industry goods, which are produced in the home as a part-time occupation primarily by members of one family using human or animal power. Handicraft goods, in contrast, are usually produced full time in a separate shop by both family members and outside labor which has been apprenticed, sometimes for up to two years' time. Thus the evolution of cottage, home, part-time production is toward small shop production. And the importance of the latter with respect to income and employment is greater than the former. In this sense, the Hymer-Resnick aggregation may not be appropriate in the context of the present paper.

8. Cf. Raul Prebisch, "The Economic Development of Latin America and Its Principal Problems," *Economic Bulletin for Latin America* (February 1962); more recently, similar criticism was made in the United Nations Conference on Trade and Development documents.

9. Y. M. Ho and D. Huddle, "Traditional and Small Scale Culture Goods in International Trade and in Employment," Discussion Paper No. 35 (1972), Program of Development Studies, Rice University; revised version forthcoming in *The Journal of Development Studies.*

10. The overall income elasticity for the eighty-one imports was 1.60120 in the U.S. time series and 1.29910 for the OECD cross-section. For LDC imports alone into OECD countries, however, the income elasticity was 2.08692 for a smaller sample of commodities. Cf. Ho and Huddle, "Traditional and Small Scale Culture Goods," tables I, II, and V.

11. Policy issues raised here are primarily based on the findings from our field surveys in Brazil, Colombia, Hong Kong, and Taiwan. Each of the above countries is interesting either from the point of view that they have serious problems in labor absorption, foreign exchange shortage, and geographical imbalance, or that they have systematically taken steps in solving those problems. Our research work described in the paper is still continuing in the countries named above.

MARKET POWER, INCIDENCE OF GOVERNMENT POLICIES, AND POVERTY: THE CASE OF FISHERMEN IN NORTHWESTERN MALAYSIA

by Marian Krzyzaniak and Uzir Malik

I. INTRODUCTION

Malaysia is a country federated at two levels. At the higher, the federation consists of peninsular or West Malaysia and Sabah and Sarawak or East Malaysia. At the lower, West Malaysia itself consists of several states (with hereditary sultans as their heads) and two federal provinces, Melaka and Pulau Pinang (Pinang Island), with governors appointed by the federal government. Since independence (1957 for the western federation and 1963 for the eastern), Malaysia has been developing speedily. In the process West Malaysia created a host of authorities, boards, commissions, research organizations, and even semi-private companies to speed up modernization of various industries, to increase production for domestic consumption and/or for export, to regulate marketing, and to set prices.

This paper focuses on the problems of the West Malaysian fishing industry in general, concentrating on the fishing industry in the so-called northern region.[1] To some degree, our analysis is also relevant for the problems of the whole West Malaysian fishing industry.

Our purpose is to evaluate the process of modernization of the industry, examining 1) how it was helped or hampered by these agencies, and 2) how the gains from modernization were shared by owners of factors employed in the fishing industry. We also submit at the end of this paper our own suggestions for a reform. We base our paper to a degree on published data and largely on interviews with government officials in various boards, bureaus, commissions, etc., in the federal capital and in second level states and provinces of the northern region. Officials of MAJUIKAN were our primary source.

The main agency to regulate and aid fishing is the (Federal) Ministry of Agriculture and Fisheries. Its main sub-agency dealing with the fishing industry is Lembaga Kemajuan Ikan Malaysia (MAJUIKAN), Fisheries

---

Mr. Krzyzaniak is Henry Fox, Sr., Professor of Economics at Rice University. Mr. Malik is Reader in Agricultural Economics at the Universiti Kebangsaan Malaysia.

Development Authority. The industry is also regulated by various second level states and provinces, and the overabundance of regulators imposes additional burdens on the industry.[2]

II. FISHING IN THE NORTHERN REGION

One peculiar facet of the West Malaysian fishing industry is its multiracial composition. Unofficial data as to the racial composition of fishermen in the northern region in 1973 are found in table 1.

TABLE 1
RACIAL COMPOSITION OF FISHERMEN, NORTHERN REGION

State	Malays	Chinese	Other	Total
Perlis	654	210	406	1,270
Kedah	4,475	1,621	27	6,123
Pinang	2,696	3,292	55	6,043
Perak*	2,441	16,800	194	19,435

*The figures for Perak show numbers of fishermen for the whole state. Presumably very few of these were living in the northern inland region.
The total of fishermen in West Malaysia was 75,486.

The races of Malaysia differ much in the size and distribution of their incomes. On the average, the Chinese have the highest income, but their income distribution is very unequal. Both Chinese and Malay fishermen are very poor.

The Malays are best organized politically. They have been able to translate their political power into legislation beneficial to them (for example, Bumiputra—native sons companies—get preferred treatment). There are no Bumiputra companies engaged in fishing, however. The Malay fishermen are numerically too unimportant to wield much political influence.

As the fishermen in West Malaysia are all very poor,[3] a purposeful state policy on behalf of this industry, were the gains from it widely shared, should contribute to racial harmony (one of the more important publicly acknowledged objectives of the Malaysian State). At present the Malaysian Chinese are, on the average, the richer, and because of this they look with suspicion at any redistributional policies of the government that in their view benefit the poorer, i.e., mainly the Malays and other Bumiputra. A redistribution policy on behalf of poor fishermen should be acceptable to each of the racial groups.

The fishing industry is of great importance to the Malaysian economy. Malaysians, though rich in resources, for various reasons do not nourish themselves properly.[4] They consume only about two thousand calories per person per day, and starches predominate in the diet. Their protein intake is especially inadequate, and the lowest levels are observed for rural Malays who for religious reasons cannot eat pork, comparatively cheaper than other meats. Thus in 1968 the non-pork-eating section of the population consumed 15.2 pounds of meat per capita per annum; the pork-eating population (mainly of Chinese descent) consumed 38.9 pounds. These figures may be contrasted with consumption of meats in the developed nations of 100-200 pounds per capita per annum.

Clearly, consumption of proteins to become adequate would have to increase at a much higher rate than the population. As fish are considered edible by all Malaysians, expansion of the fishing industry should have a high priority. At present fish catches amount to 330,000 tons; other meats and eggs supply only 147,335 tons.[5] A small quantity of fish is exported; the value of this export is large enough to pay for fish imported by Malaysia, making West Malaysia self-sufficient in production of fish proteins.

In the past, both fresh- and salt-water fishing were done commercially in Malaysia. In the northern region, the major areas of fresh-water fishing were the mud flats of the Muda River valley. There (after the monsoon season) rice was grown, but off-season fishing was an important activity.[6] As Malaysia was a net importer of rice, the federal government decided to irrigate the Muda valley, so that two crops of rice a year could be harvested there. At a substantial cost to the treasury, the irrigation scheme was successfully executed, and Malaysia became nearly self-sufficient in rice production;[7] in the process, however, production of fresh-water fish in the area was destroyed.

Fortunately, expansion of fishing in the straits of Melaka turned out to be possible, and the increase in salt-water fishing more than offset the loss of catch in the Muda River flats. Upswelling currents in the Melaka straits bring deep-sea nutrients into shallower waters, which turn into breeding grounds and teem with valuable fish.

Because of a moderate incline of the sea bed, the straits fishing grounds can be divided into four categories. 1) There is a shallow offshore strip where the more valuable fish breed. Any commercial fishing there would be destructive to this national Malaysian resource. The Malaysian states and provinces, therefore, forbid commercial fishing in a strip extending seven miles from the shore. 2) Further away, the straits for miles are shallow enough to permit commercial bottom fishing. This is a highly profitable operation, but these grounds are limited. An element of monopoly has to be introduced by the states (provinces) to protect them from overfishing. 3) As the sea gradually deepens, one has to change from bottom to sea level fishing, but farther from the shore cutters and trawlers used for fishing must be larger than near-shore vessels to be seaworthy. In other words, such fishing must become more capital-intensive. 4) Finally, Malaysians could undertake ocean fishing. This requires large capital investment in ocean-going fishing ships, and so far Malaysia has not created such fleets. As Malaysians are, historically, experienced seafarers, this development remains a potentiality not to be overlooked when expansion of fishing becomes a national necessity.

Fishing offshore of West Malaysia is further complicated by the sea laws that limit national control of the seas. Until such laws are changed, much of Melaka straits is also open to fishing by other nations, especially by the Japanese, the Burmese, and the Thai. Indonesian fishermen are not a problem since they still have much of their own offshore waters to develop.

After the Malaysians switched to more salt-water fishing, it soon became clear that the profitable bottom fishing in the straits of Melaka is a limited resource, vulnerable to over-fishing. There are, however, problems involved in protecting the straits. Legal regulations cannot be made flexible enough. Specifically, the fish breeding grounds do not coincide with the seven-mile offshore limit on fishing and often extend further than that. Valuable young fish often go into the zone where bottom fishing is permitted, and get caught there, as may be seen from the high percentage of trash fish often caught by bottom fishing methods.[8]

To avoid the constraint, Malaysia may further develop its fishing on the eastern shores of West (peninsular) Malaysia and on the northern shores of East (Timur) Malaysia, i.e., off the island of Borneo. This, of course, would benefit fishermen living near such coasts but will not help the fishing industry in the northern region. The distances make such fishing unprofitable for the northern region fishing fleets.

The only reasonable way to protect the fishing in the straits is by regulation. We have already mentioned the prohibition of commercial fishing in the seven-mile offshore strip. More important has been restriction of the numbers of fishing licenses issued by the states. Given the small size of boats in the straits, license restriction effectively restricts the size of the catch, protecting the straits from depletion. Unfortunately, this environmental measure is equivalent to a government monopoly of fishing rights.

The question was, who was to receive the monopoly rents from fishing in the straits? Federal or state governments could have operated the industry as a monopoly but decided not to. Still, they could have tried to reap the monopoly rent by auctioning fishing licenses. Whether they would have been successful we shall never know, because auctions of licenses were not tried.[9]

Instead, governments charged moderate fees for operating fishing equipment and fishing boats, foregoing collection of monopoly rents from fishing.[10] A redistributional decision had to be made. Licenses could have been issued to fishermen organizations (co-ops or partnerships), an action which would have alleviated the abject poverty of this group, but such a policy to be successful would require provision of capital as well to the fishermen. To avoid this cost the states issued licenses not to fishermen but to financiers, who were able to provide the boats and finance the operations themselves. As straits fishing has been very profitable, the financiers were most willing to buy licenses and organize the fishing. The uneducated and miserably poor fishermen had no alternative but to join as hired crews.

III. THE FISHING INDUSTRY IN PINANG AND LANGKAWI ISLANDS

Better to understand problems of the fishing industry in the northern region, we paid special attention to sea bottom fishing in the straits of Melaka by two groups of fishermen: those of Pinang and those of the Langkawi Islands.

In the Pinang area, bottom fishing (seven miles offshore) is done by trawlers of ten to twenty ton capacity with crews of four fishermen (including the captain). Up to 280 fishing licenses are granted to financiers who supply the boat, hire the crew, and advance operating costs (fuel, ice, etc.). The trawlers use Batu Maung on Pinang Island as their port, but neither do the fishermen live there nor do the buyers of fish have their offices there. The latter live and operate in Pinang City (some financiers, themselves, are fish buyers). After each catch, trawlers return to Batu Maung, the fish are classified as trash fish (from 40-50% of the catch) or human-consumption fish and divided by type into separate baskets. The crew does not have any means to weigh the fish nor any idea of prevailing prices paid that day by the fish buyers. The trash fish are taken by a trustee of a fish cooperative to which the financiers belong.[11] The valuable fish are taken by the financier to Pinang and the next day the crew is told the value of its share in the catch. From the total value obtained by the financier (according to his account), the first M$200 is subtracted to cover his expenses and the remainder divided in two, half for the financier, half for the crew. The average income of an able fisherman (one share) comes to about M$100 per month, but wages may vary around the average. The captain and the first mate usually get one and a half shares; in addition, the captain may also get a commission if the catch is good. The low income of fishermen is partly due to a large content of trash fish in the catch. Insofar as trash fish includes young valuable fish that prefer coastal waters, one suspects that many crews may be breaking the law by fishing too close to the shore for prawns. Such practices damage the ecology of the straits, depleting them of future mature human-consumption fish.

Clearly, the low incomes of Pinang fishermen are a result of their weak market power.[12] They have no boats of their own, hence can only be hired hands. The law, by selling licenses to financiers, favors the latter. The crew has no control over the sale of its catch, does not know the weight, does not know what prices are in fact obtained, or whether or not the fish are sold to the highest bidders. The marketing of trash fish is of little value to the crew, who get only 2 cents per kati (one kati weighs 1.33 pounds) for it.

Some crews, infuriated by their low incomes, strike back. They are tempted to sell part of their catch for cash on the seas to foreign ships, pocket the proceeds, and bring back only the remainder. If the financier suspects the crew, he can sack them, but with little confidence that his next crew will be any better. Lately, some of the financiers have put a trusted man (often a family member) among the crew. In any case, the risk involves some costs and these increase the need for a larger margin to the financier. Although it is the system under which the financiers operate that causes the need for controls, it is the consumer who pays, in higher prices of fish.

Prices of fish delivered to the port (hereafter called "ex boat") are difficult to establish, for there are no published statistics. Averages can be obtained from MAJUIKAN officials but only for their operations at Langkawi Islands. To get some idea about ex boat prices at Batu Maung we visited the port and interviewed several fishermen leaving boats for home. They claimed that often their catch of valuable fish brings them only ten Malaysian cents per kati on the average. Given the sharing system, this figure translates into twenty-five Malaysian cents ex boat per kati. This, of course, is only the lower limit of the ex boat price range. Against this one may consider the whole spread of retail fish prices per kati in Kuala Lumpur, which runs from 45 cents for small Chencharu, to M$2.60 for Bawal Puteh, to M$3.48 for medium prawn (all these quotations are for the first quarter of 1973). Clearly, the average margin over ex boat prices is not as large as the figures compared here might indicate, but it is substantial.

At Langkawi MAJUIKAN (Alor Star Branch) started a very interesting experiment. It bought twelve trawlers (thirty-ton capacity), hired crews of six for each trawler, and now runs them somewhat along the lines of the private operations at Pinang. There are, however, differences, and the most important is that MAJUIKAN has a subsidiary company in Pinang that buys fish and pays better prices than private buyers. Specifically, we found that in a particular (considered representative) catch the ex boat average price per kati was 91 cents, almost four times the above-quoted lowest price of 25 cents.

The captain of the crew also gets a small commission from MAJUIKAN's share if the catch is good. Finally, 10% of fishermen's income (shares) is banked at interest and is available only in case of emergency or at retirement. In the MAJUIKAN operation the amount of trash fish is smaller, representing only 10-15% of the catch. Despite this, the average income of an able fisherman is only slightly higher (M$120 per month) at Langkawi than at Pinang (M$100 per month). The reason is that some boats have small catches or high repair and maintenance costs. One must also suspect inefficiency or cheating (selling on the high seas).[13]

IV. FISH MARKETS

The fish markets in western Malaysia are oligopolistic, and we suspect a high level of collusive behavior among the financiers organizing the industry.[14] The monopolistic powers of the latter are strengthened by government limitations on issuance of licenses for bottom fishing and transfer of the resulting monopoly profits to financiers already engaged in the industry. To compound the inequitable distribution of the value added in the fishing industry, markets in which fish are sold are far from competitive. This is not a peculiar feature of fish marketing alone. Many other industries in Malaysia have a similar problem.

In general, specialized wholesalers create their own networks of buying agents and of retailers. Members of these networks are tied to the respective wholesalers by financial arrangements (credit). Insofar as most of the wholesalers are of Chinese descent, the network has its ties further strengthened by consanguinity (members are either relatives or at least members of the same Chinese clan). Above all, network ties are strengthened by collusive behavior among the wholesalers themselves. Any retailer who might refuse to accept a delivery because his wholesaler overcharges him would be cut off from further supplies by him, and no other wholesaler will deal with the "rebel."

Further proof of oligopolistic structure and collusive behavior of wholesale fish markets is based on price behavior. Official data for the first quarter of 1973 quote fish prices for several regional markets.[15] Three will interest us here: Pinang Island, Ipoh, and Kuala Lumpur. Only Pinang Island is in the northern region, but the market at Ipoh in the state of Perak draws perhaps some fish caught in the region. Both markets also export fish to the national capital in Kuala Lumpur, hence our interest in this third market.

The data seem to support the claim that there is no national market in fish in West Malaysia if we define *national market* as one in which regional market prices usually differ only by the cost of transporting a given good from the exporting to the importing region, plus a normal profit. Shipping cost of a pikul (100 kati, or 133 lb.) of fish from Pinang or Ipoh to Kuala Lumpur, with cost of ice added, could not exceed M$10, and adding a margin for profit and weight loss from evaporation, wholesale prices at Kuala Lumpur should not be more than M$20 (per pikul of any kind of fish) higher than the price in the exporting region. We find, however, that in the first quarter of 1973 the market price differential was about M$50-60 and, in the case of prawns, about M$100 or even more. One must presume that such price differentials are representative of wholesale fish market operations in West Malaysia. If the markets were competitive, some wholesalers could bring the cheaper fish into Kuala Lumpur and force prices down greatly. As that does not happen, one must presume that wholesalers do not need to fear such imports and (being stocked with high priced fish) keep the old price until the stocks are gone. This is compatible with profit maximization but markets are then monopolistic or collusively oligopolistic. For the Malaysian people this has meant high prices to consumers in Kuala Lumpur, low prices to fishermen in Pinang and Ipoh. Only the wholesalers in Kuala Lumpur are protected from the consequences of their overstocking with fish, for which both the primary producers and final consumers have to pay.

MAJUIKAN is aware of great imperfections in Malaysian fish markets and is in the process of forcing fish auctions. The auction system is not yet operative in the northern region. Whether this measure by itself will bring substantial competition to fish marketing remains to be seen. Probably many additional measures need to be taken concurrently before competition in wholesale markets is enforced.[16]

V. EVALUATION

We have shown in the preceding sections that:

1) The market for fisherman labor is oligopsonistic. The financiers hire crews as if they all were representing one employer. The hand of financiers is further strengthened by a) existence of collusive practices, perhaps arrived at and enforced by the so-called fishing cooperatives (in fact trade associations of the financiers), and b) existence of governmental monopoly through issuance of a limited number of licenses for sea bottom fishing. As Malaysian governments did not try to extract the resulting monopoly rents for themselves, and issued licenses to previous licensees, profits of the latter must have increased and stabilized at such higher levels.

2) The market for fish is also oligopolistic, concentrated in the hands of a few wholesalers who are also able to tie some of the financier boat owners directly to themselves.[17] Because of high levels of collusion in both markets, "monopoly" and "monopsony" models describe these markets fairly well.

3) Poorly educated fishermen have no incentive to switch jobs, because unskilled labor in other fields is equally ill-paid. Therefore, the labor supply for fishing remains inelastic.

The concentration of market power in both markets resulted in low wages for Malaysian fishermen, and in general in very unequal distribution of incomes out of value added by the fishing industry.

Although it is difficult to evaluate the effect of concentration and monopolization, in this case our estimate is that the decline in fishermen wages was steep; the latter probably got only half the wage they would have received had the markets been competitive.

Clearly Malaysian fishermen do not get their proper share in gains from economic development. Market imperfections explain this to a degree, but governments by their desire to protect environment contributed also to the weakening of fishermen's economic position. A monopoly of fishing rights in the straits of Melaka has been created, and the resulting monopoly rents have been inadvertently passed to financiers.

VI. POLICY PROPOSALS

The fishing industry of West Malaysia—especially in the northern region—is in a precarious position. It is a major producer of protein supply in a nation starved for proteins; but its most profitable form (bottom fishing) cannot be expanded, at least in the straits of Melaka, for environmental reasons. Its "monopolistic-monopsonistic" nature also makes the industry inefficient and produces great income inequality. Thanks to the preponderance of the market intermediaries and financiers, the fishermen themselves are kept abjectly poor, but consumer prices are high. The basic objectives of the government should be to bring more competition to fish marketing and to reorganize the industry in general, so that a more equitable distribution of incomes will result.

Bringing competition to fish marketing in Malaysia will not be easy. Many other industries of Malaysia suffer the same problems. So far, governmental solutions have taken the form of regulation of marketing, mainly through the licensing of agents, both buyers and sellers. Licensing, however, only substitutes private monopoly for public and does not assure operating at purely competitive prices.

MAJUIKAN wants to impose auctioning of fish in public, regulated markets. Such would appear to be a step in the right direction, but one doubts whether this measure alone could restore competition. A more basic restriction of competition is hidden in the tying of retailers and purchasing traders to a single wholesaler. Tying to a wholesaler firm, enforced by collusion with other wholesalers, is mainly responsible for the present structure of fish and other produce trading in Malaysia.

To break the ties between the retail and wholesale trade, positive steps will be needed. Introduction of vigorous trading cooperatives might be one, but so far in Malaysia such cooperatives have atrophied in this function. Development of supermarkets might help. Some state-supported development of refrigerating and freezing units might also bring price stability and less spoiling of fish. Also more competition might result if information about market conditions is more widely disseminated. Perhaps publicly operated scales at ports would help. The fish buyers might be issued licenses only if they open offices at the fishing port (perhaps only three fishing ports are needed in the northern region: at Batu Maung, Kuala Kedah, and Langkawi). They should post their prices each day so that the crews may know them in advance, or at least at the time the financier takes over the catch. Also, the fishing licenses of any Malaysian state should not restrict selling of the fish exclusively to ports of the state issuing the license. Elimination of this restriction might prevent unneeded costs and make fish buyers more competitive.

The second major objective should be reorganizing the industry itself. The task should be comparatively easy because the lack of market power of fishermen is attributable mainly to human causes. Clandestine collusion among financiers should be made illegal. Specifically, the present fishing cooperatives should be disbanded and replaced by a single fishing cooperative whose membership is open to all crews. The trash fish should be sold by this cooperative at auctions to fish meal operators, and the proceeds after cost credited to crews according to their catch of trash fish. The licenses to fish should be given to crews or their captains, and not to financiers (the boat owners would then hire only fishermen with licenses to fish).

A major step in giving the fishermen market power would be dispersion of ownership of boats. Ideally the smaller boats should belong to the crews (preferably partnerships or small cooperatives) or to individual captains. A start can be made by changing the MAJUIKAN experiment in the Langkawi Islands. At present MAJUIKAN forces the employed crews to save by banking a small part of their earnings. The savings could be increased by adding captains' commissions (the latter perhaps even doubled to give captains an incentive to produce good catches). MAJUIKAN could permit withdrawal of savings for the purpose of buying boats, and could also auction its older boats used at the Langkawi Islands experiment to fishermen (but not to financiers).

If such a policy becomes successful, the government could initiate low interest state loans to the fishing crews so that they may buy boats belonging to financiers in Pinang.[18] The laws supporting "Bumiputra" (native sons) firms could be appropriately extended to fishing.

The reforms proposed here need not be construed as inimical to financiers. Their capital could be reinvested in ocean going fishing ships for which licenses should be issued to financiers as well as to any applying captain, and the Malaysian state could give tax incentives in such cases (as it does now to many other "new" industries).[19]

As for the monopoly rents from issuance of a limited number of licenses to bottom fishing boats, there are two alternatives to the present system of passing them to the financiers. They could be extracted by auctioning licenses, but that would make development of fishermen-owned fleets difficult. Perhaps for the time being such monopoly rents should not be extracted by the states, but passed to crews with licenses. This would speed up the process of developing fishermen owned fleets; and only after a transitional period should the matter be reconsidered.

NOTES

The authors wish to thank the Economic Planning Unit (hereafter called E.P.U.) at the office of the Prime Minister of Malaysia in Kuala Lumpur for giving its support and facilitating contacts with Malaysian officials in various branches of Malaysian governments, and to thank the latter for giving generously of their time and information. The authors alone are responsible for the use of the information. Special thanks go to the Faculty of Economics and Management at the Universiti Kebangsaan Malaysia at Kuala Lumpur for providing space and facilities.

1. The northern region, as defined by authorities, consists of states—Perlis, Kedah, northwestern part of Perak—and the province of Pulau Pinang (including the Island of Pinang and the former [continental] province of Wellesley). Apparently the Federal government of western Malaysia is worried about the lagging development and the increase in income inequality in this region. The National Action Committee set up the Northern Malaysian Regional Action Committee, giving the Economic Planning Unit (E.P.U.) the task of preparing policy proposals and coordinating the workings of this body.

2. One cause of the "excess" is the federal structure of West Malaysia. The provinces, states, and the federal government all have a role. Licensing belongs to the state or province. These usually require that licensees sell the fish in provincial markets. Thus, if a boat is on high seas and the captain wishes to sell the catch, the boat has to return to its base, even if other ports are closer and offer higher prices for fish. Such a regulation unnecessarily increases costs (diesel fuel burned, time lost) and decreases the revenue (price obtained).

3. For data and need of redistribution, see Donald R. Snodgrass, "The Fiscal System as an Income Redistributor in West Malaysia," *Public Finance* **29**, no. 1 (1974): 58. According to Snodgrass, the mean household income per month in West Malaysia in 1970 was M$267, while the mean income of fishermen's households in 1973 or 1975 would be half of that or less. Income inequality in West Malaysia is high. Snodgrass estimates the Gini coefficient to be .502.

In 1974 the U.S. dollar exchanged for about 2.40 Malaysian dollars, but the purchasing power of the Malaysian dollar was higher, about equal to 75 U.S. cents.

4. See Anuvar bin Mahmud, "Food Problems in Malaysia," *Food Problems in Asia and the Pacific,* Proceedings of a seminar held at East-West Center, Honolulu, Hawaii, May 1970.

5. Ibid. See especially p. 192, table 2.

6. See "The Boom Which Turned into an Avoidable Slump," *Malaysian Business* (February 1975): 8-17.

7. At present Malaysia is almost self-sufficient in rice (thanks to Muda Valley Irrigation Scheme), fish, pork, and poultry. Beef must be imported, as must maize, soy beans, etc. There are some exports of tapioca and tropical fruits, but other fruits have to be imported. For data on Malaysian exports and imports see: Ministry of Agriculture and Fisheries, *Statistical Digest,* 1966-1971, pp. 78, 92, 93, and 94; and Federal Agricultural Marketing Authority, *Quarterly Commodity Statistics* **4**, no. 1 (Jan/March 1973).

8. Trash fish consists of inedible fish (for example, starfish), damaged fish, and fish that are too small to be eaten. In the latter category one may find a substantial fraction of young fish, valuable when grown, but the method of bottom fishing does not permit removal of it from the catch and return to the seas alive. Some catches bring as much as 40-50% of trash fish. The closer to shore one fishes by bottom fishing methods, the more low-priced trash fish will be caught. On the other hand, high-priced prawns abound in coastal waters. Coastal police have caught numbers of commercial boats fishing in the forbidden zone. A high percentage of trash fish in the catch thus raises suspicion that the boat was poaching, though it was lucky to escape apprehension.

9. In the Malaysian economic climate, owners of capital (mainly people of Chinese descent and foreigners) are accustomed to formation of rings, cartels, and all sorts of collusive organizations. It is, therefore, likely that auctions alone could have failed to collect monopoly rents for the states from fishing.

10. Two types of fees are charged. One schedule sets fees for use of fishing equipment (First Schedule—Regulation 5). One has to pay M$2 per annum for four bag nets, the same for gear of barrier nets, draft nets, set of hooks and traps, etc. Fishing stakes cost from M$10 to M$50 per gear; trawl nets, depending on the horsepower of the boat, cost up to M$50.

Fees are also required for operating a boat. The fee varies according to the month of the year in which the license is bought and the horsepower of the vessel. Maximum charge is M$35.

These clearly are moderate fees and in real terms have declined since inflation hit Malaysia badly in 1973-74.

11. There are eleven such cooperatives but a lesser number of trustees because several cooperatives have the same person for trustee. The trash fish is sold for about 4½ cents per kati (1.33 lb.). Given the sharing agreement between the financier and his crew, this means 2 cents per kati of trash fish to the crew.

"Fishing cooperative" is a misnomer. They are not true cooperatives because the existing membership must agree by a two-thirds majority vote to take in a new member. Also the members are not fishermen, but financiers. Fishing cooperatives seem to be clubs or trade restraining associations, strengthening the position of the financiers against the fishermen.

12. We argue later (see section v) that in the absence of the monopolistic power of wholesalers and with competition in fish marketing, fishermen's wages could have been double what they were actually paid.

13. To prevent this either the crews could be sacked or an informer system organized and the guilty crews brought before the courts.

14. The published statistics have little to offer in terms of analysis of structures in the markets. *Census of Wholesale and Retail Trades in the Urban Areas of Peninsular Malaysia, 1970* (Kuala Lumpur, Malaysia, 1974), table 2, p. 2, states that in the urban areas of peninsular Malaysia there were 456 wholesale establishments trading in fish. Clearly, this is rather a large number; not only numbers but organization of markets counts, however, and that is not well documented in published statistics.

First, the fish markets, as will be shown later, are regional—not national—and it is the smaller number of such firms in each regional market that is relevant. Second, the wholesale trade is heavily concentrated among the Chinese, who (as is well known) often enter into trade combines because they belong either to the same clan or to the same trade association.

Establishment of trustees to sell trash fish by the eleven fishing cooperatives in Pinang (see also note 11) is a clear sign of open collusion in marketing of fish. We suspect that these trade associations are also a vehicle for other more clandestine collusive arrangements (for example, setting local industry-wide conditions of employment of hired labor). We noted that some financiers are also buyers of fish.

15. See *Quarterly Commodity Statistics* **4**, no. 1 (Jan/March 1973).

16. We are not very optimistic that adequate and appropriate measures will be taken. In the past, Malaysian governments reacted to lack of competition in trading by licensing. This may have helped to break the ties between various levels of trading, but it resulted in more monopoly rather than less. Substitution of private monopoly by bureaucratically enforced monopoly seems to solve nothing. The monopolistic exploitation power is then strengthened, not weakened.

17. We noted that in Pinang many financiers are tied to particular wholesalers, or are themselves fish buyers. To unravel the mystery of who in the Chinese community owns what is *per se* a difficult task, and as it was not our objective we left it to future researchers of the Malaysian economy.

18. At present fishermen in search of credit may depend only on meager savings of close relatives and on advance wages from financiers organizing fishing trips. The latter source decreases further any market power fishermen may have retained.

Thus, the only source of organized credit could be the (state) Agricultural Bank which distributes its credit through cooperatives. Unfortunately, the cooperative movement in rural Malaysia is very weak; whatever exists is very bureaucratic, and fishermen do not belong to existing fishermen cooperatives.

19. Thus the development of fishing activities may be assigned to the already existing agency called PERNAS.

REFERENCES

1. *Census of Wholesale and Retail Trades in the Urban Areas of Peninsular Malay, 1970.* Kuala Lumpur, Malaysia: Department of Statistics, 1974.

2. Mahmud, Anuvar bin. "Food Problems of Malaysia." *Food Problems in Asia and the Pacific.* Proceedings of a seminar held at East-West Center, Honolulu, Hawaii, 1970.

3. *Quarterly Commodity Statistics.* Farm Agricultural Marketing Authority **4**, no. 1 (January-March, 1973).

4. Snodgrass, Donald R. "The Fiscal System as an Income Redistributor in West Malaysia." *Public Finance* **29**, no. 1 (1974): 56-76.

5. *Statistical Digest.* Ministry of Agriculture and Fisheries, 1966-1971.

6. Unsigned article, "The Boom Which Turned into an Avoidable Slump." *Malaysian Business* (February 1975): 8-17.

III

INTERNATIONAL ISSUES

THE DISTRIBUTIONAL IMPLICATIONS OF THE TAXATION OF NATURAL RESOURCES

by Malcolm Gillis and Charles E. McLure, Jr.

I. INTRODUCTION

Few economic events of the early 1970s have attracted more attention than the large increases in taxes or quasi-taxes levied upon primary products, especially natural resources, by a small number of countries that control large segments of world markets for these commodities. The most important case, of course, is petroleum. The actions of the Organization of Petroleum Exporting Countries (OPEC) have caused chaos in the economies of developed as well as developing nations, and may yet wreck the international monetary system. Even worse, many already desperately poor countries have been further impoverished by paying higher prices for imports of primary products, particularly fossil fuels. Of course, we tend to think of the gains from the increases in taxes as accruing primarily to the low-density countries of the Middle East, many of which already enjoy extraordinarily high per capita incomes. But several poor countries such as Indonesia and Nigeria have also been able to improve their economic status at the expense of the developed countries—although also at the expense of other poor countries—so that the tax increases do not necessarily make the worldwide distribution of income less equal.

Looking with envy at the success of OPEC and other earlier, but less spectacular, instances of cooperative action by producer countries, other countries have sought to duplicate the success of these cartels, in commodities ranging from bananas to mercury and copper.[1] The success or failure of such further efforts to form cartels will, of course, have distributional implications roughly similar to those of the OPEC cartel. The colluding countries will improve their positions at the expense of either consuming nations or creditor nations if they are successful in shifting the new taxes from their own people to people of other countries. Many, but not all, of the producing countries are in the developing world, and most of the nations that supply

---

Mr. Gillis is Institute Fellow in the Harvard Institute for International Development and Lecturer in Economics at Harvard University. Mr. McLure is Allyn R. and Gladys M. Cline Professor of Economics and Finance at Rice University.

capital are in the developed world. Thus backward shifting of the taxes to owners of capital would generally tend to equalize the worldwide distribution of income. On the other hand, as noted above, consuming nations are both rich and poor, so that forward shifting to consumers has less clear-cut distributional effects. But one thing stands out in the discussion to this point. If we are to know how the taxes under discussion affect the worldwide distribution of income, we must know their incidence, that is, whether they can be shifted, and in which direction.

We propose some guidelines based on economic analysis of the determinants of the incidence of taxes on natural resources and other primary products. In section II we discuss the conditions under which various kinds of taxes on primary products can be shifted forward and backward to nonresidents of the taxing nations. Then in section III we apply the framework developed earlier to analyze one specific case, beginning with the large tax Jamaica imposed upon bauxite in the summer of 1974. We believe that the general framework and this example will assist the reader in appraising the likely incidence of various other taxes on primary products (or the chances of success of other attempts at cartelization).[2]

II. THE GENERAL DETERMINANTS OF INCIDENCE

Table 1 (p. 149) presents the general determinants of the incidence of taxes on natural resources. Because this table and its explanation employ a bit of the economist's shorthand notation, it seems convenient to digress from the main subject long enough to explain a few of the terms used in this table and the remainder of the paper.[3]

A. Definitions

Resource rents are earned by owners of an asset (such as a natural resource) that is provided by nature and that has no alternative use.

Differential resource rents exist when favorable conditions such as low transportation costs, ease of extraction of the resource, high quality ores, etc., result in higher resource rents than are generally available.

Quasi-rents are earned on capital that is invested in some activity, and that, being specific to such use, has no alternative use in the short run. In the long run, as capital depreciates and funds become available for other investments, they will be employed in activities in which it is expected that they can earn a *normal return.* If an investment is particularly good, the resulting quasi-rents exceed normal returns during the subsequent short run, but if the investment is less successful (or is rendered so by tax policy) quasi-rents can fall below the normal return expected when the investment was undertaken.

Finally, *monopoly rents* occur when barriers to entry into an industry allow the firms already in the industry to charge prices high enough to earn extraordinarily high returns on their investments, even in the long run, because of the lack of any threat of competition from new entrants. Monopoly rents are found more frequently in *oligopolistic industries*, in which a few firms dominate an industry, than in the relatively rare cases of non-governmental pure *monopoly*, in which there is but one firm in the industry.

B. Market Dominance

The first determinant of the ability to shift taxes on natural resources is the position of the taxing nation or nations in the relevant market for the taxed resource. One nation producing a small portion of the world's supply of a mineral, for example, could not hope to export a tax on that mineral to nonresident consumers through higher prices, because the world price would be almost totally unaffected by the nation's imposition of the tax. Rather, the tax would reduce returns to producers of the mineral in the short run and perhaps render production unprofitable in the long run, as discussed further below. On the other hand, a nation or group of cooperating nations responsible for the entire world production of a product might be able to shift a substantial portion of any tax on that product to consumers in other countries. Of course, the most common cases are in the middle ground of partial dominance, since few, if any, important products are completely dominated by one country and cartels are at least as difficult to organize and maintain among countries as they are among firms.[4] Finally, we must note explicitly that the relevant market for a commodity may not always be easy to demarcate, because of the presence of substitutes of various degrees of perfection. As we shall note below, for example, aluminum may be easily replaced by glass and steel in the container market and is competitive with copper in the electrical industry, but has no rivals in the production of aircraft.

C. Mobility of Factors

If capital is not mobile out of a taxing country, or even out of a taxed industry within the country, it is essentially earning quasi-rents, according to the definition given in part A of this section. In such a case, any tax that cannot be shifted simply reduces these quasi-rents and is borne by investors in the taxed industry. If, on the other hand, capital is mobile, either out of the taxing nation or out of the taxed industry, it can largely escape the tax. Since much mining and refining equipment is not easily transferred to other domestic uses and since it is often difficult or prohibitively expensive to dismantle such machinery and move it out of the taxing nation (even if the nation would permit such a response to its tax policy), the question of capital mobility basically hinges on whether we are discussing the short run or the long run of economic theory. Whereas in the short run capital is fixed and earning quasi-rents, in the long run depreciation of facilities generally renders capital mobile.[5]

Labor may also be relatively immobile in response to taxes that are shifted backwards to it, for several reasons. For example, a certain group may, by tradition, work in the mines and mills of a country and continue to do so even following a tax-induced reduction in wages. Other cultural factors, such as geographical preferences or discrimination in other occupations, may limit groups to the taxed industries. In such cases these workers are essentially immobile and, like the owners of immobile capital, they earn quasi-rents, rather than wages determined competitively in the nationwide market. A somewhat different situation occurs in those instances in which unionization has resulted in workers receiving wages above the competitive wage rate. In such cases the worker is not immobile in quite the same sense as in the previously discussed case, but the results are similar: the worker is receiving a form of monopoly rent and will not, within limits, leave the industry even if his wage is reduced somewhat by the backwards shifting of the tax levied on his employer.[6]

Finally, we should note that in most cases the natural resource is itself highly immobile in the sense that it may have little alternative use. To the extent that this is true, the resource is earning resource rents which are a highly vulnerable target for countries wanting to raise additional revenues, perhaps at the expense of nonresidents, while avoiding undesirable economic consequences. As noted below, the type of tax, the economics of transporting the resource, and institutional factors are important determinants of the extent to which a given tax will come to rest on resource rents.

D. Industrial Structure

The incidence of a particular tax is likely to depend in important ways upon the extent to which the market is dominated by a few firms, as well as the extent of dominance by taxing countries. In particular, a tax levied on a competitive industry by dominant nations is more likely to be shifted in full to consumers than is a similar tax levied upon a monopolist. The reason for this apparently anomalous result is that the monopolist would presumably have maximized his profits in the absence of the tax. In that case, part of the tax would cut into his monopoly profits, rather than being shifted to consumers. In general we expect that about half the tax would come out of profits and only about half would be reflected in higher prices.[7]

Of course, as suggested above, monopoly is rare, and in the world of natural resources, perfect competition is, too. The more common form of industrial structure is oligopoly. Unfortunately, economic theory can tell us little about the price response of an oligopolistic industry to an increase in the taxes it pays—or more accurately, it can tell us just about anything, depending upon the assumptions we make about the behavior of the firms (that is, upon which theory of oligopoly we accept). This is not the place to attempt a taxonomy of the many theories of oligopoly and their implications for tax incidence.[8]

Rather, we simply note that if the industry has maximized the joint profits of its member firms, the results will resemble those of the monopoly case, but if it has not, the results will be more like those of the competitive case.[9]

Finally, as noted above, unionization may result in workers receiving a form of monopoly rent. But unionization and industrial concentration tend to go together. Moreover, multinational firms tend to pay more than the local wage rate, even in the absence of union pressures, in order to reduce turnover, avoid labor discontent, etc. Thus workers may be sharing in the monopoly and resource rents of their employers.

E. Type of Tax

Taxes and quasi-taxes on natural resources can take a multitude of forms, but we shall restrict our attention to two general forms: the production tax and the income or profits tax.[10] The production tax, if levied by nations that dominate the market, would be shifted forward in large part. On the other hand, if it were levied by a non-dominant nation, the tax would be likely to reduce the quasi-rents of owners of immobile capital in the short run. It would tend to discourage continuation of production in the taxing nation in the long run, unless there were some mitigating factor such as differential resource rents that could be tapped through backward shifting. Of course, it is possible that some of the burdens on capital would be shared by labor specific to the taxed industry.

The situation is somewhat different where income taxes are concerned. For one thing, there are problems of the transfer price appropriate to use for intra-firm transactions in calculating taxable profits (especially those of multinational firms) that are less critical in the case of production taxes. Second, from a theoretical point of view, the incidence of profits taxes is considerably more uncertain than is that of production taxes. Beyond that, income taxes are levied on the entire return to capital, including normal returns to equity capital, as well as pure profits (monopoly rents, in the present discussion). Thus these taxes are likely to have economic effects somewhat different from those of a tax on pure profits. In particular, to the extent that the tax drives the return to equity capital below what can be earned on alternative investments, it, too, would discourage investment in refining in the taxing nation, even though in the short run it would merely reduce the various rents. Finally, foreign tax credits are generally available only for income taxes. As long as income taxes do not exceed amounts allowed as foreign tax credits by capital-exporting nations, those nations bear the full burden of income taxes levied by the natural resource-producing nations. Similarly the existence of full crediting reduces the amount of tax that must be borne by either consumers or recipients of factor incomes. Therefore, in what follows we consider only income (profits) taxes (and other taxes) that are not credited.

F. Final Considerations

Several additional determinants of the incidence of taxation of natural resources do not fit easily into the taxonomy of table 1, and would make it undesirably complicated, even if they did. For example, it matters greatly whether contractual arrangements can be altered in response to changes in tax policy. Examples of contracts that might be altered are labor contracts, supply contracts, lease arrangements, etc. Moreover, it is important to know whether the natural resource can be exported for processing elsewhere if local processors attempt to shift taxes backward to the mining stage. In some cases economic considerations, especially weight loss and costs of transportation, dictate on-site processing, but in others they do not. In addition, there may be restrictions on the export of unprocessed natural resources, especially if the country is experiencing severe problems with excess capacity in its own processing plants. The importance of the resource cost in the total costs of final products is an important determinant of the possibilities of shifting a tax forward to consumers. Clearly the tax can be shifted more easily if the resource is a relatively minor component of the cost of final products. Beyond that, the existence of differential resource rents is an important determinant of whether heavy taxes can be levied without rendering the industry economically non-viable in the taxing nation. A final consideration is purely mechanical. Once we have identified the consumers and factor owners who bear the various taxes we must allocate the taxes to their nations of residence.

G. The Taxonomy

If we ignore severance taxes, suppress repeated mention that labor may share in the burden of some taxes (especially in unionized industries and in industries with substantial amounts of resource rents and monopoly rents), and ignore the existence of differential resource rents, we can identify the twelve cases presented in table 1. As in the previous discussion, we distinguish between the owners of resources and the capitalists who exploit the resources and process them, though the two groups may, in reality, be largely the same in many cases. The first group receives resource rents, including differential resource rents. The second receives normal returns to capital in the long run, quasi-rents in the short run, and perhaps monopoly rents.

Case 1: Production taxes levied on competitive industries by nations dominating the world market for a resource would be shifted in large part to consumers, if capital is mobile. In each case examined, income taxes would be borne by owners of natural resources to the extent that they applied to resource rents. But that part of income taxes falling on the normal return to equity capital would be likely to be shifted to consumers, since any tendency to reduce the return to capital would result in capital being invested in other industries, perhaps in other countries.

TABLE 1
GENERAL DETERMINANTS OF THE INCIDENCE OF TAXES ON NATURAL RESOURCES

I. Market dominance by taxing nations	Yes		No	
II. Capital mobility from taxed sector	Yes	No	Yes	No
III. Industrial structure				
a. Competition	1	4	7	10
b. Monopoly	2	5	8	11
c. Oligopoly	3	6	9	12

Case 2: Only about half of the production tax levied on the monopolist would be shifted to consumers, even if the taxing nations dominated the market. The remainder would be borne by recipients of monopoly rents. To the extent that it applied to economic profits, the profits or income tax would be borne by capitalists. To the extent that the tax hit the normal return to capital, the result would be similar to the analogous part of the tax in the competitive industry. The existence of monopoly rents in the taxed industry might make that industry more attractive than other investment opportunities, however, so long as the tax does not completely offset that attraction. Thus in a particular case it is important to know the magnitude of the monopoly rents in the industry and to compare them with the size of the taxes tending to reduce the return to capital.

Case 3: As suggested earlier, the results for oligopoly are likely to resemble those for either monopoly or competition, depending upon the extent to which profits of the industry have been maximized in the absence of the tax.

Cases 4-6: With capital completely immobile, a tax either on production or on the profits of refiners is likely to be borne by recipients of quasi-rents and, where relevant, by recipients of monopoly rents. Given existing patterns of ownership of processing capacity, such a tax would result in substantial amounts of short-run exporting of taxes to capitalists in developed countries. Thus in either the long run or the short run nations that dominate world markets for important products are likely to be able to export taxes on those products. But the implications for the worldwide distribution of income are somewhat different in the two cases. In the short-run (capital immobile) case the primary burden is likely to be on capitalists, a group which can be characterized with reasonable accuracy as the upper income groups in the developed nations. But in the long run the burden comes to be borne increasingly by consumers, that is, by lower income groups in the developed nations and in increasing proportions by citizens of the poorer countries.[11]

Case 7: In this case a country that does not dominate the world market levies a tax on processing of a natural resource, even though the capital employed in the processing industry is mobile. Because of non-dominance the tax cannot be shifted to consumers, and because capital is mobile neither form of tax can reduce the normal return to capital, which in a competitive industry is the only return capital receives. If the taxed resource cannot be exported in unprocessed form, say because of transportation costs or government regulations, the tax may be shifted backward to owners of the natural resource. But if the resource can be exported for processing elsewhere, the tax may well destroy the refining industry in the taxing nation. If this occurs, the burden of the tax may fall largely upon labor, due to the reduction in the country's capital-labor ratio and the need to absorb the released labor elsewhere.[12]

Case 8: This case is remarkably similar to the competitive case. Economic theory tells us that profits are maximized when marginal cost (the incremental cost of producing a unit of output) equals marginal revenue. But if the taxing nation does not dominate the world market, marginal revenues are determined in the world market. Thus the tax has no effect on the profit-maximizing price and is therefore not shifted to consumers. And because capital is completely mobile, by assumption, the tax cannot reduce the normal return the monopolist receives, though it may reduce monopoly rents. Thus in this case, as in case 7, either a processing tax or a profits tax on processing will tend to depress the processing industry in the taxing nation, unless conditions are such that it can be shifted backward to owners of natural resources or that it simply reduces monopoly rents.

Case 9: As in cases 7 and 8, either tax would be borne by recipients of resource rents (and perhaps labor) if conditions allowed, and would tend to destroy the industry if not.

Case 10: The price of output is determined in world markets, because of non-dominance, and capital is fixed in supply to the taxing nation, and therefore earning quasi-rents. Either a production tax or a profits tax reduces those quasi-rents. Of course, this is only short-run analysis, and it is to be expected that in the long run the results will be as described in case 7.

Cases 11 and 12: These cases have results similar to those in case 10, with the added feature that monopoly rents will be reduced as well. The important distinction between these three cases and the three previous cases is that the passage of time tends to concentrate the burden of the tax upon workers and owners of resources as capitalists remove (or threaten to remove) their processing facilities in response to a tax that makes their continued investment in the taxing nation unprofitable. This may or may not result in a more progressive domestic tax burden and increased exporting of the tax, depending upon the patterns of incidence and the ownership of the natural resources and processing facilities. But because dominance is necessary (if not sufficient) for shifting tax burdens to consumers and because ownership of both resources and processing facilities is concentrated in the developed countries, it is virtually certain that taxes levied by nondominant nations will have a more egalitarian effect on the worldwide distribution of income than those levied by dominant nations. Finally, it appears that cases 1 through 3, in which we find both market dominance and factor mobility, are quite different from cases 4 through 12. In the first group of cases consumers, including those in poor countries, are likely to bear a considerable burden of any taxes on natural resources. In the other cases the absence of either market dominance or capital mobility, or both, results in difficulties in shifting either a tax on production or a tax on profits in the processing industry forward to consumers. To the extent that capitalists and owners of resources are concentrated in the developed countries and in the upper income classes in all countries, natural resources taxes levied in the context of cases 4 through 12 are likely to make both the distributions of income within countries and the worldwide distribution of income more equal.

III. THE BAUXITE CASE

From 1901 through 1936, there were six major cartel agreements between companies in the international trade of aluminum, all of which seem to have been successful in raising prices significantly above what would have been expected in the absence of the agreements.[13] Until 1974 there were no examples of international commodity agreements or cartel-like arrangements in bauxite, the principal ore from which aluminum oxide (alumina) is refined for later smelting into aluminum ingot. In March 1974, however, seven major bauxite producing nations (Australia, Guinea, Guyana, Jamaica, Sierra Leone, Surinam, and Yugoslavia) took the first formal steps, in Conarky, Guinea, for establishing the International Bauxite Association (IBA). By November 1974, the IBA was fully established, with permanent headquarters in Kingston, Jamaica, and three new members (The Dominican Republic, Ghana, and Haiti) had been admitted to membership.[14] The only significant developing-country producer still outside the IBA fold is Indonesia, whose 1973 production was about 2% of world mine output.[15]

Although the members have steadfastly avoided using the "cartel" label for IBA, and have not yet taken simultaneous coordinated actions, the goals of IBA (securing higher revenues from bauxite and alumina and developing vertically integrated aluminum industries in member countries) are not atypical of past cartels formed by producing firms. Following the initial IBA meetings, however, Jamaica announced in May 1974 unilateral actions designed to expand its bauxite revenues by U.S. $170 million per year, or about 50% of total tax receipts for 1973-74. The measure served to raise the nation's tax revenue (exclusive of royalties of U.S. $0.55 per ton) from bauxite from about $1.34 to about $10.50 per ton, an increase of almost 700%. The government also announced its intention to secure a sizable increase in participation in the bauxite and alumina operations of the large international aluminum firms present in that country, which together hold under lease or ownership some 1.5 billion tons of bauxite reserves, or over 80% of estimated Jamaican reserves.[16] Because of the difficulty of determining profits attributable to operations in Jamaica, the new tax was levied on production, rather than on profits. And because of the difficulties in determining an arms-length or free market price for bauxite, the tax was geared to the price of aluminum ingot (7.5% of the realized price, as determined by the government, on shipments of primary aluminum for 1974-75, to rise in steps to 8.5% by 1976). Finally, to forestall the possibility that the aluminum companies might counter by reducing production, the tax was based on a presumed minimum level of production equal to somewhat over 90% of estimated production.

Within two months of Jamaica's unilateral actions, Guyana announced virtually identical taxes,[17] and the Dominican Republic was considering similar measures.[18] Surinam implemented changes nearly matching those of Jamaica in mid-December 1974, enacting taxes of about $10.00 per ton, retroactive to January 1, 1974.[19] Finally, in early 1975, Guinea and Haiti imposed stiffer bauxite levies modeled along the lines of the Jamaican measures.[20] Of the ten IBA members, only Australia, Sierra Leone, and Yugoslavia had refrained, as of this writing, from announcing tax increases on a scale comparable to the Jamaican levies. (But the executive board of IBA intends to forge a common pricing formula for bauxite by no later than November 1975.)[21]

There is little doubt that the Jamaican government, as well as the governments of other IBA members which followed the Jamaican initiative, expected the increase in the tax to be borne by foreigners. In this section we utilize the conceptual framework developed in the previous section to determine whether this is a reasonable expectation. The focus is, naturally enough, upon the existence of market dominance and upon the presence of resource rents, quasi-rents, and monopoly rents. It will be convenient to reverse the order in which industrial structure and capital mobility are considered.

A. Dominance

Aluminum is the most plentiful metal found in the earth's crust (8% of the earth's crust by weight) and occurs in bauxite and all clays.[22] Aluminum-bearing materials other than bauxite have not been extensively exploited, however, as their low aluminum oxide content (and/or high silica content) relative to the bauxite deposits found in IBA nations has rendered derivation of alumina from these materials a much more costly proposition.[23] Bauxite is still the cheapest source of aluminum, but known world reserves of bauxite are sufficient to support 268 years of world aluminum needs at 1973 levels of production, so that the ore hardly qualifies as an example of "rare earth." Fully 63% of world bauxite reserves, however, are located in the territory of the original seven IBA members, who also accounted for 62% of world mine production in 1973. The U.S. has only about 1% of world bauxite reserves,[24] while other non-communist nations outside of IBA account for less than one third of world reserves and less than one quarter of 1973 production. Australia alone accounts for 30% of world bauxite reserves, followed by Guinea at 23% and Jamaica at nearly 7%. Within IBA, three of the ten members are responsible for a heavy share of total world production. In 1973, Australia (23%), Jamaica (20%), and Surinam (10%) accounted for 53% of world mine production (see table 2).

TABLE 2
WORLD BAUXITE PRODUCTION 1973
(Percentage of Totals)

I. *IBA Members*	*68.7*
1. Australia	22.7
2. Jamaica	20.0
3. Surinam	9.9
4. Guyana	5.1
5. Guinea	4.3
6. Yugoslavia	3.2[a]
7. Sierra Leone	1.0[a]
8. Other IBA members (Haiti, Ghana, Dominican Republic)	2.5[a]
II. *Rest of World*	*31.3*
1. Indonesia	1.8[b]
2. U.S.S.R.	6.9
3. France	4.5
4. United States	2.7
5. Other nations	15.4

[a]Authors' estimate.

[b]Department of Mining, Republic of Indonesia.

SOURCE: Unless otherwise indicated, *Commodity Yearbook*, 1974.

The four largest producers of bauxite have a particularly strong position, especially in their primary markets, even without the support of other IBA members. The Caribbean producers in general enjoy an especially advantageous position in the U.S. market. Jamaica and Surinam alone accounted for 75% of U.S. bauxite imports in 1973. For the period 1968-1972, the four most important Caribbean producers (Jamaica, Surinam, Guyana, and the Dominican Republic) accounted for fully 91% of U.S. imports of bauxite, or about 80% of U.S. mine production plus imports.[25]

These facts, and others considered briefly below, suggest that IBA nations can export a substantial portion of their recent increases in taxes on bauxite. Most obviously, tax exporting to foreign consumers may be possible at least in the short- to medium-term. This conclusion would be strengthened by Australian support of common pricing formulas favored by other IBA members, but may be weakened by considerations of industrial structure.[26] Perhaps equally important, locational and other advantages of the Caribbean deposits create important differential rents that are particularly vulnerable to appropriation through fiscal measures.

Although Jamaican deposits contain only 50% alumina (about equal to that of much of the Australian and Indonesian deposits), they enjoy significant advantages of physical accessibility, low silica content (bauxites with low silica content are the cheapest to process by the Bayer method) and low transport costs. Guyana's deposits are less accessible (owing to a heavy overburden of sand and clay). The alumina content of Guyana's ore (57%) is the highest in the world for major deposits, however, and the country has a virtual monopoly on calcined bauxite (used in the abrasives and refractory industries). Discovery and exploitation of sizable new bauxite fields of comparable quality and accessibility does not appear likely to exert significant downward pressure on differential resource rents of Caribbean deposits through the medium term. The few known large, unexploited deposits are distant from the markets of Jamaica, Guyana, and Surinam (and are located in other IBA nations, or in nations likely to join IBA, such as Indonesia).

The nature of alumina refining—which involves substantial weight reduction (typically 50%)—also generates differential locational rents, above those accruing to bauxite deposits, as such. Recent and projected increases in shipping costs are expected to increase the premium for processing alumina near extraction sites.

B. Industrial Structure

The international aluminum industry is dominated by six major producers (Alcoa, Alcan, Kaiser, Reynolds, Pechiney, and Alusuisse), who together held 66% of the net equity ownership of western capacity (1970) in primary aluminum[27] and an undetermined but probably equally large share in net equity in bauxite mining and refining. The six major producers are all fully integrated from bauxite to metal and are active in mining and processing activities throughout the world, often through joint ventures with one another and with smaller companies. American and Canadian firms have a relatively greater role in the Caribbean, European firms tend to dominate in Africa, and nearly all have substantial investments in Australia and the Far East. Concentration in aluminum smelting has declined since 1950.[28] But the substantial economies of large-scale production at this stage, in which (before the energy crisis) 60% of total aluminum cost was incurred, still work to the advantage of the major producers. The six major firms control 80% of western-world primary aluminum capacity, about half of world trade in bauxite, alumina, and aluminum, and a large share of fabrication capacity.[29] Given the preponderance of the majors at all stages of bauxite-alumina-aluminum markets and their predilection for cooperative behavior, which is facilitated by participation in joint ventures among the six, it is hardly arguable that substantial potential exists for monopoly and monopsony rents from Caribbean mining activity. The existence of monopoly rents, of course, reduces the possibility of shifting to consumers, but increases that of exporting the tax to non-resident capitalists.

C. Capital Mobility

In the short run quasi-rents accrue to the multinational firms engaged in the mining of bauxite or the refining of alumina. The package of inputs earning quasi-rents includes not only capital, but the associated technological, management, and (often) labor skills required for modern, capital-intensive mining. Given the longevity of the substantial amounts of capital invested ($800 million in Jamaica, for example[30]), the "short run" of economic theory may turn out to be lengthy, and the appropriation of quasi-rents could be the vehicle of considerable tax exporting. In addition, several of the major international firms have invested heavily in alumina refining in IBA nations. As most of these refineries are designed to process specific grades of bauxite, adapting them to different grades of bauxite, not to mention non-bauxite aluminum-bearing materials, would require large investments. Thus capital invested in alumina refining is not likely to be highly mobile. But while the multinational firms can do little in the short run to combat the reduction of their quasi- (and other) rents,[31] in the long run they can move, especially if the tax policies of the bauxite-producing nations are not fully coordinated. Whether in the long run capital is driven out depends in large part on whether (and the extent that) increased taxes on bauxite go beyond the mere capturing of differential resource rents plus a portion of monopoly rents, and encroach upon the normal return to capital and technical knowledge and skills.

D. Other Considerations

1. Ordinary Demand and Cost Considerations

The recent fiscal measures enacted by the bauxite producing nations of the Caribbean provide a good example of the importance of being unimportant. Bauxite costs as a proportion of ingot costs (before 1974) have been placed at 10%, while the costs of refining alumina and smelting are 18-20% and 60-70%, respectively.[32] Therefore, the Jamaican tax increase would, if fully passed forward, raise ingot prices by only about two cents per pound, or by 6% over prices prevailing in July 1974.[33] Whether a price increase of this magnitude would induce substantial short-term shifts away from aluminum, the second most used metal in the U.S., is difficult to determine.[34] The conductivity, strength-to-weight, corrosion-resistance, and formability of aluminum suggest that existing substitutes, such as steel, copper, and plastics, would not be likely to make substantial inroads into aluminum's markets. Costs of replacing aluminum in transport and electrical applications would be particularly high, although substitution could easily be achieved in the beverage and container industry (16% of the aluminum market). Finally, scrap supplied about 19% of total U.S. aluminum production in 1972-73.[35] Tax-induced increases in aluminum prices could spur recycling efforts, but this is quite a limited source of supply, except in the short run.

Probably the major source of concern for the Caribbean members of IBA is the possibility of longer-term displacement of bauxite by other aluminum-bearing materials in abundant supply in the U.S. and elsewhere in the developed world. The U.S. is rich in aluminum-bearing clays, such as nepheline synite, and has substantial deposits of alunite and anorthosite. But the alumina content of these ores is, at between 30% and 38%, significantly lower than that of most Caribbean, and for that matter, most IBA deposits (except the low silica deposits of trihydrate bauxite in Australia, with an alumina content of 35%). Furthermore, from all accounts the technology for extracting alumina from non-bauxite materials is still in the pilot-study stage. The U.S. also has very large dawsonite resources, contained in the same formations as oil shale in the Rocky Mountains. If the U.S. were to opt for a policy of extracting oil from shale, dawsonite (with an alumina content of 35%) would be a sizable by-product, and could supply the world's aluminum needs for decades. The possibility of competition from dawsonite would seem to pose little threat to IBA members, however, at least at present tax levels. On the contrary, if IBA members were convinced that the U.S. intends to exploit its oil shale reserves, they would be well advised to raise taxes on bauxite even further, in order to extract the maximum rents before large-scale generation of dawsonite or dramatic technical change in aluminum refining and smelting renders their bauxite deposits worthless.[36]

2. Type of Tax

As noted earlier, Jamaica, Guyana, and other IBA members levied higher production taxes, rather than profits taxes, on bauxite producers. This is rather difficult to explain, since foreign tax credits are generally available only for income taxes. But beyond that, it is necessary to notice that the Jamaican tax is no ordinary production tax in that it presumes a minimum level of production. Thus it is in effect a lump sum tax if production falls below the stipulated level and is truly related to production only after the presumed minimum is surpassed. This feature prevents the majors from holding Jamaica hostage by temporarily shifting production to their mines in other countries and thereby depressing the Jamaican economy. To the contrary, Jamaica in effect is holding the firms hostage. As the tax must be paid, whether bauxite is mined or not, the only economical thing to do, for the time being, is to mine at least the minimum level stipulated by law.

E. Summary

Jamaica and other Caribbean members of IBA effectively dominate the North American bauxite market and are behaving in a consciously parallel, if not collusive manner. IBA members as a whole could dominate the world bauxite market if Australia should fully support IBA goals. Moreover, the industrial structure is oligopolistic. Thus in the short run, in which capital is essentially immobile, we are dealing with case 6 of our conceptual framework. Over the long run, market dominance may weaken (if the tax ultimately renders Caribbean or other IBA bauxite non-competitive) or it may increase (if IBA becomes a strong worldwide cartel). Thus, in the long run we are dealing with either case 3 or case 9. In case 3 we would expect substantial (say 50-100%) shifting to consumers; depending upon the behavior of the oligopolistic firms that dominate the world and U.S. markets, substantial short-run shifting to consumers might occur even in case 6. Recipients of resource and monopoly rents would bear the remainder of the burden in these cases, and they and recipients of quasi-rents would bear the full burden if case 9 turns out to be relevant. Given consumption patterns and the effective ownership of the major aluminum firms and Caribbean bauxite deposits, there seems to be little doubt that substantial amounts of the new bauxite taxes can be exported in both the short run and the long run, subject only to constraints imposed by weakness of the IBA and (if IBA proves to be impotent) the level of differential resource rents.

Whether the IBA will be a viable cartel is, of course, unpredictable. And because of the lack of generally recognized arms-length prices for bauxite, it is not possible without further detailed analysis to determine precisely whether the recent tax increases in Jamaica and other IBA nations have served to wrest away the entire amount of differential resource rent accruing to their bauxite deposits. Similarly, it is also impossible to determine the size of monopoly rents in mining activity, because of the complexities of marketing and pricing and the nature of oligopolistic interaction between multinational enterprises. But the behavior of several of these firms provides some operational evidence that in fact Jamaica, Guyana, Surinam, and others have not gone too far—and perhaps that the major aluminum producers expect the IBA to achieve its objectives cooperatively. Although all the firms operating in Jamaica filed arbitration requests with the International Center for Settlement of Investment Disputes (ICSID) immediately after the tax increase, within six months one of the largest (Kaiser) not only agreed to abandon ICSID proceedings against Jamaica, but assented to the government's purchase of 51% of the firm's bauxite mining assets.[37] In return, the company will receive a guarantee on reserves sufficient to maintain current rates of extraction for thirty years. Though Kaiser has geographically less diversified holdings of bauxite than the other majors, and was therefore under more pressure to settle, this action was nonetheless a significant development.

A few months after preliminary negotiations with Kaiser were completed, another major company, Revere, settled with the Jamaican government on much the same terms as established for Kaiser, and also agreed to expand its alumina capacity on the island by nearly three-fold.[38] The Revere agreement was followed in April 1975 by a settlement between Reynolds Aluminum and the Jamaican government. Like Kaiser, both Revere and Reynolds agreed to sell to the government 51% interest in the companies' mining operations, and both agreed to withdraw proceedings from ICSID.[39]

The last two of the North American companies operating in Jamaica, Alcan and Alcoa, had not come to terms by May 1975. Because Alcoa depends on Jamaican bauxite for only 17% of its aluminum production—much less than the producers who have already agreed to Jamaican government terms—it will probably be the last company to reach an agreement, if indeed it decides to remain on the island.[40]

NOTES

1. The analysis in the remainder of the paper refers to taxes imposed on various products or on the profits earned in extracting or processing the products, even though in many cases we are dealing with higher royalties, governmentally posted prices, marketing boards, etc., rather than with taxes *per se*.

2. One of the responses to OPEC's actions has been for petroleum-producing states in the United States to raise their taxes on the production and/or refining of petroleum products in an attempt to capture some of the windfall gains generated by the higher prices for oil and petroleum products, or to export some of the higher taxes to residents of other states. The analysis presented here is of direct relevance in the appraisal of the likely economic effects of such taxes.

3. These concepts are explained more fully in Helen Hughes, "The Distribution of Gains from Foreign Direct Investment in Mineral Development," Southeast Asia Development Advisory Group, Asia Society, SEADAG Papers on Problems of Development in Southeast Asia, 74-10 (New York, 1974).

The theoretical underpinnings for the analysis presented here are contained in Charles E. McLure, Jr., "Commodity Tax Incidence in Open Economies," *National Tax Journal* **17** (June 1964): 187-204; "The Interstate Exporting of State and Local Taxes: Estimates for 1962," *National Tax Journal* **20** (March 1967): 49-75; and "General Equilibrium Incidence Analysis: The Harberger Model after Ten Years," *Journal of Public Economics* **4** (1975): 125-161.

4. We ignore the possibility of coordinated action by consumer nations against producer nations. Given the large number of nations that would have to cooperate if such action were to be effective, and the rewards from being outside a buyers' cartel in the event of economic warfare between consumers and producers, it seems unlikely that cooperation among consumer nations will be an important influence in determining the ultimate incidence of the taxes under discussion.

5. Of course, for the purpose of this analysis, if equipment can be transferred to alternative uses or shipped to countries in which its output is not subject to tax, it is mobile. On the other hand, even in the long run capital may be essentially immobile if repatriation of funds is blocked by exchange controls and if investment must be maintained in the taxed industry whether or not it is optimal, or even profitable, for the firm to do so. These qualifications illustrate the necessity of detailed analysis of individual cases.

6. Labor may also share in the burden of taxation, even if it is mobile and labor markets are competitive, if the tax results in the release of labor from the industry and the labor cannot be absorbed into the remainder of the economy without depressing wage rates. The extent to which this occurs depends upon the relative importance of the natural resources sector in the total economy, whether capital is also shifted to the remainder of the economy, the factor proportions (capital/labor ratios) in the various sectors, and the ease of absorbing labor into the remaining sectors, as indicated by elasticities of substition. In what follows we shall ignore this complicated qualification, even though in many cases it may be quite important.

7. For more detailed explanations of this result, see, for example, Richard A. Musgrave and Peggy Musgrave, *Public Finance in Theory and Practice* (New York: McGraw-Hill, 1973), pp. 433-434 and 436-438; and (at a somewhat more advanced level) Richard A. Musgrave, *The Theory of Public Finance* (New York: McGraw-Hill, 1959), pp. 287-299. Briefly, the argument is that the tax moves the monopolist away from the price that maximizes profits. Roughly one-half of the tax is reflected in reduced profits, rather than in either higher prices or lower costs.

8. The interested reader is referred to Musgrave, *Theory of Public Finance,* chapter 13, for a survey of the subject; and to William Fellner, *Competition Among the Few* (New York: Knopf, 1949), for a more detailed survey of oligopoly models. Among the more interesting and potentially important aspects of this subject, and ones that are seldom discussed in theoretical analyses, are the relations between firms and nations. Firms might, as they did in Jamaica, band together in the effort to prevent increases in taxes. Or they might encourage nations to raise taxes. It has been suggested, for example, that the latter course was followed by the international oil companies, since a higher price for OPEC oil would increase the value of the firms' reserves in the United States. The question is beyond the scope of this paper, though the analysis presented here should prove useful in isolating instances in which firms would act in the two ways just described.

9. In certain cases one or a few purchasing firms acting cooperatively may dominate the market for the output of a country or group of countries. The incidence of taxes levied on such monopsonistic firms can be analyzed using theoretical constructs similar to those used in the

analysis of monopoly. A firm which was monopsonistic in input markets but sold in competitive output markets would, as in the monopoly case, bear about half the burden of the tax. But in this case the remaining half of the burden would be borne by resource owners, rather than by consumers. A firm that was both a monopolist and a monopsonist could shift about half of the tax in each direction, but would nonetheless suffer a reduction in profits. Finally, as is true on the product side, oligopsony (few buyers) is more common than monopsony. But the theory of oligopsonistic behavior is even less developed than that of oligopoly behavior. Given the tendency for collusion among firms in input markets to give way to competition, and the rarity of pure monopsony, we ignore the possibility of monopsony in what follows.

10. We treat export and production taxes together, since for practical purposes they generally have similar distributional effects. A third type of tax, the severance tax, is imposed upon the removal of the natural resource from the earth. To the extent that the resource can be extracted with little marginal cost, such a tax cannot be shifted by the owner of the resource. If nonresidents own the resource, most of the tax will be exported. But costless extraction is unusual, and the production-profits distinction will suffice for most purposes.

We use the term "owner" to identify the persons or organizations who have economic interests in the resource during the relevant period of time. This may, of course, be someone who has leased the mineral rights from the actual owner. But the legal owner would have an economic interest in the resource if the rental payments were based on value of production.

11. The observant reader might reasonably ask how this conclusion squares with the earlier statements—and the observable reality—that the OPEC increases in oil were shifted to consumers. The problem is that the price increases were really increases determined by a group of colluding owners of resources who had not previously maximized their joint profits, and not taxes *per se*. Furthermore, the quasi-taxes are more like severance taxes than like refining taxes. If present prices maximize profits and if the resources in question were owned by some third party, further increases in the taxes would be borne primarily by the owners of the resource, rather than being shifted forward.

12. Note that in this case the tax might have an appreciable burden, even if it yielded little revenue. In fact the welfare loss could greatly exceed the amount of revenue generated.

13. The criterion of "success" here is whether or not the organization was able to raise prices at least 200% above the unit costs of production and distribution and keep them there for a significant period of time (about two years). See Paul A. MacAvoy, "A Review of Research Findings on the Longevity of International Cartel Agreements," unpublished memorandum, October 1974, p. 1 and appendix.

14. United States Department of the Interior, Bureau of Mines, *Mineral Trade Notes* **71**, No. 12 (December 1974): 29.

15. Departamen Pertambangan, Republik Indonesia, *Pertambangan Indonesia,* 1973, p. 104.

16. M. Manley, "Statement Before the Parliament of Jamaica on Current Bauxite Negotiations," May 15, 1974.

The international firms are Alcan, Alcoa, Anaconda, Kaiser, Reynolds, Pechiney, and Alusuisse.

17. Guyana's tax was set at about 6% of the aluminum ingot price. Given the higher aluminum oxide content of Guyana bauxite, the production tax per ton of bauxite virtually matched that of Jamaica. The December Surinam measures clearly had the same intent.

18. *New York Times*, July 11, 1974. The Dominican Republic finally secured the agreement of Alcoa on higher bauxite levies in December (*New York Times,* December 21, 1974, p. 41).

19. *New York Times,* December 21, 1974, p. 41.

20. *Financial Times,* March 11, 1975.

21. *Wall Street Journal,* April 23, 1975, p. 7.

22. A. M. Bateman, *Economic Mineral Deposits* (New York: Wiley, 1950), p. 213.

23. Aluminum oxide content of Jamaican and Australian bauxite deposits is about 50%; Arkansas bauxite reserves contain 40%-60% alumina, while the aluminum oxide content of Guyana ore is about 57%. The typical aluminum oxide content of bauxite exports from Indonesia, a non-IBA member, is 53.5%. Aluminum oxide content of typical non-bauxite aluminum-bearing materials (anorthosite, alunite, dawsonite, kaolin-type clays) runs from 25% to 45% *less* than most bauxite found in IBA nations, although low-silica Australian deposits of bauxite with alumina content of only 35% are now mined. See U.S. Department of the Interior, *Commodity Data Summaries,* Washington, D.C., 1974, and Departamen Pertambangan, *Pertambangan Indonesia,* p. 101.

24. *United States Mineral Resources,* Geological Survey Professional Paper No. 820 (U.S. Government Printing Office, Washington, D.C., 1973).

25. U.S. Department of the Interior, *Commodity Data Summaries,* 1974, pp. 15-16. IBA members also accounted for over 95% of 1973 U.S. imports of alumina, with the greatest share (57.4%) coming from Australia, followed by Jamaica (26.8%) and Surinam (11.3%).

26. Australian spokesmen in IBA have indicated that that nation will have to study any common pricing proposals "very carefully" (*Wall Street Journal,* March 10, 1975, p. 16). Whether or not any common policy on pricing could, in the medium to long term, be effective without Australian support, is an open question.

27. R. A. McKern, *Multinational Enterprise and National Resources: A Study of Foreign Direct Investment in Australian Mining Industry* (unpublished D.B.A. thesis, Harvard University, 1972), Appendix A, p. 76.

28. Raymond Vernon, "Competition Policy Toward Multinational Enterprise," *American Economic Review* **64** (May 1974): 276.

29. McKern, *Multinational Enterprise and National Resources,* Appendix B, p. 73.

30. North American Aluminum Producers in Jamaica, Press Conference, New York, May 16, 1974.

31. Indeed, a phased withdrawal from Jamaica would appear to be ruled out by the minimum tonnage provisions enacted in May. See *Metal Bulletin,* No. 5954, January 3, 1975, p. 19.

32. McKern, *Multinational Enterprise and Natural Resources,* p. B-76.

33. International Economic Policy Association, *U.S. Natural Resource Requirements and Foreign Economic Policy,* Washington, D.C., July 1974, p. 82.

34. According to the Department of Interior figures (*Commodity Data Summaries,* 1974), U.S. demand for aluminum increased 18% in 1973, and world demand also increased dramatically in the face of rising world prices. On the other hand, American and world demand sagged badly in the last half of 1974 and first quarter of 1975, and producers' primary aluminum inventories in February 1975 stood at 89% above February 1974 levels (see *Wall Street Journal,* April 23, 1975, p. 5). But it cannot simply be assumed that this is a result of the taxes. Demand for aluminum is strongly cyclical and would normally be adversely affected by world recession. In fact, the industry apparently believes that present market weakness may last until October 1976, after which users may face several years in which the metal will be in short supply (see *The Economist,* March 1, 1975, p. 64).

35. *Commodity Data Summaries,* p. 2.

36. Recognition of the future threat to bauxite from technological progress apparently figured heavily in the Jamaican decision to opt for drastic increases in taxes on bauxite in 1974, rather than phasing in increases in taxes over a longer period. The Jamaican Prime Minister was

explicit on this point in May 1974: "If present reports are correct, the time may not be too distant when technological progress will begin to yield substitutes for bauxite" (Manley, "Statement Before the Parliament of Jamaica," p. 2).

37. *Financial Times*, November 22, 1974.

38. Ibid., March 6, 1975, p. 23.

39. Ibid., April 15, 1975, p. 24.

40. Ibid., March 6, 1975, p. 23.

COMMODITY AGREEMENTS AND THE NEW INTERNATIONAL ECONOMIC ORDER

by Gordon W. Smith

Support for fundamental changes in international commodity markets has swelled considerably since 1973. Among others, Prime Minister Harold Wilson, the European Economic Community, and the United Nations Conference on Trade and Development (UNCTAD) have advanced their general plans for reform, and the United States is expected to do so shortly.[1] Several factors explain this rather sudden about-face by many governments. First, there was the commodity boom and bust of 1972-1975. Raw materials prices soared to unprecedented heights and appeared to lead the double-digit inflation which plagued most industrial countries. Then many commodity prices collapsed in late 1974 and 1975, leading to fears that future supplies would again be inadequate. Surely, many feel, something can be done to reduce such wild gyrations in prices (see figure 1).

Second, the so-called "Third World," strengthened by short-run commodity shortages, began to push much harder in the United Nations and other organizations for a "New International Economic Order." The New Order proposals start from two assumptions. 1) The current international economic system is heavily biased against the less developed countries (LDCs) and tends to retard their development. 2) The rich nations of the world have a duty to make far greater sacrifices than hitherto in order to alleviate the plight of the poor nations. A brief (not inaccurate) summary of the policy conclusion drawn from these assumptions is that in all international economic dealings, preferential and non-reciprocal treatment should be given to LDCs. In the law of the sea, for example, this would mean that LDCs would be the primary beneficiaries of deep sea mining. In international finance, LDCs should be the main (initial) recipients of new special drawing rights, the International Monetary Fund's "paper gold." In international trade LDCs should be given special tariff preferences. Technology should be transfered to LDCs on very favorable terms; and in primary commodities, our main interest here, the New Order would mean much higher, more stable raw materials prices, indexed to the costs of LDC imports from the industrial countries.[2]

Mr. Smith is Associate Professor of Economics at Rice University.

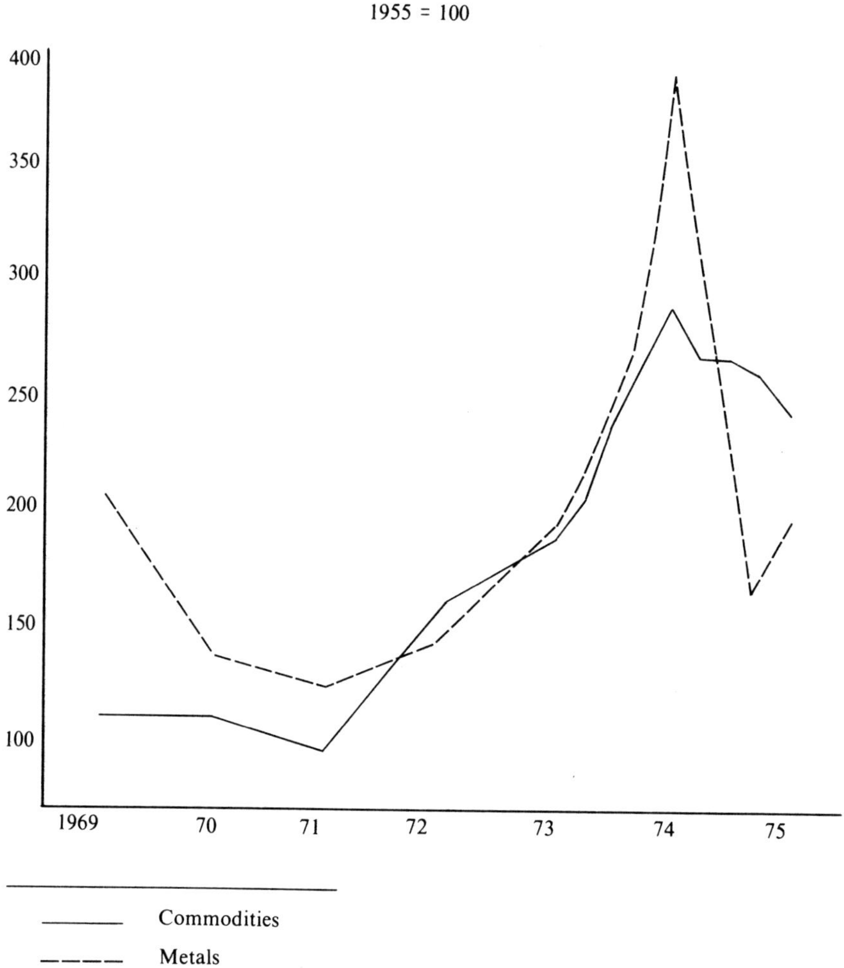

FIG. 1. *THE ECONOMIST*'S PRICE OF RAW MATERIALS 1969-1975.

In more "normal" times, the industrial nations probably would have listened politely to such demands and then ignored them as they had so often in the past;[3] now the Organization of Petroleum Exporting Countries (OPEC) has successfully tied the discussion of oil to that of other raw materials. The industrial countries can no longer be sure that refusal to yield on the raw materials front will not lead to retaliatory actions in oil.[4] Hence, many consuming nations have become much more "forthcoming" in other commodities than they otherwise would have been.

In addition, there has been much concern that producer cartels might form in commodities other than oil, and that OPEC money might be used to bolster their probability of success.[5] This fear was intensified by a proliferation of "producers associations" in raw materials ranging from iron ore, bauxite, and copper, down to tungsten. In most cases cartel-type action has not yet resulted from producer efforts, and calmer analysis since mid-1974 has led most observers to discount considerably the probability of successful cartels in all but a few commodities. Still, the threat cannot be dismissed entirely and is one motive for the change of heart in some of the developed countries.

Clearly the goals of the industrial nations in proposing new commodity arrangements are quite different from those of the LDCs. The industrial countries all want to avoid a repetition of the shortages of 1973. They want to forestall the development of producer cartels, and they want to assure an abundant, secure, long-term supply of raw materials. Some of those concerned also hope that pressure by petroleum suppliers might be relaxed somewhat in exchange for concessions by the developed countries in regard to other raw materials. Finally, most DC governments are seeking political good will with the LDCs, which they hope will spill over to favorable treatment in areas other than commodities.

The strong LDC demand for higher, and indexed, commodity prices, is unlikely to be accepted voluntarily by the industrial nations. The claim that raw material prices are "too low" goes at least as far back as Raul Prebisch's 1949 thesis that there is a long-run tendency for the terms of trade—export prices/import prices—to turn against raw materials exporters. Since there is no valid economic justification for the alleged tendency, Prebisch and his supporters in UNCTAD have concluded that it results from the exercise of some kind of "monopoly power" by the industrial countries. Accepting the premise, LDCs demand redress in the form of permanently higher prices.

Statistical evidence has never been decisive in the debate about the terms of trade. Even after a group of experts, convened by UNCTAD itself in late April 1975, agreed unanimously that the pertinent statistics did not provide any clear evidence of a long term deterioration in the net barter terms of trade of developing nations, New Order advocates persist in their assertions.

In any case, Third World demands for permanently higher and indexed raw materials prices would require the end of international markets as they currently operate. Supplies would have to be lowered below market equilibrium levels, and mechanisms to guarantee the restriction would have to be created. Export or production quotas would be necessary in many countries, and cooperation of the importing nations would be required to prevent extensive cheating. The problem of *quota allocation* is extremely difficult. Usually quotas have been determined by past production or export performance.[6] This procedure tends to freeze the pattern of production, and in the case of many minerals, where new discoveries are occurring constantly, quotas ultimately would generate gross distortions in the location of production.

Indexation would compound the problem. Indexation links a price or another monetary value to some general index of prices, normally as an adjustment for inflation. Escalator clauses which tie wages to the cost of living index are probably the most common example, although some countries also index the face value of government bonds and other financial assets. Rigid indexation of commodity prices, however, makes little economic sense. It would lock in relative prices at levels which could rapidly become unsupportable without the kinds of controls discussed above. The resulting misallocation of resources could be serious, while the technical obstacles to calculating "appropriate" price indices for the indexation procedure are formidable indeed.

For these "technical" reasons alone, there is very little chance that the industrial countries will agree to enforce higher than equilibrium prices in world raw materials markets. Nor, in spite of the rhetoric, is it clear that many LDCs realistically expect them to agree.

This does not mean that nothing constructive can be done on the raw materials front. To the contrary, both groups of countries would seem to have a mutual interest in attacking the extreme price *instability* plaguing many of the industrial raw materials. For many LDCs, unstable commodity prices translate into very unstable and unpredictable export earnings, often upsetting all attempts at consistent and rational economic planning;[7] but the industrial countries also lose from extreme price instability. Uncertain cash flows probably reduce the level of investment and production in raw materials ventures. Furthermore, raw materials price swings tend to aggravate the underlying inflationary and recessionary forces in the industrial economies. This has been most apparent in the 1972-1975 period, when raw materials prices exploded in the face of fears that supplies were reaching the point of nonavailability (see figure 1).

At this point, the perceptive reader may ask why there is a problem at all. Private market speculation should be able to take care of price instability, at least to the extent that is socially desirable. The speculator could buy and store in times of low prices and sell in times of high prices. As long as the price rose over the holding period more than the speculator's interest, storage, and other costs, he could make a profit; and if the speculator could not show a profit, the degree of stabilization achieved would cost more than it was worth socially.[8] This line of reasoning has a certain appeal; but one thing is patently clear—private speculators have not in fact done a particularly good job in stabilizing the prices of industrial raw materials.

The reasons seem fairly straightforward. Future expected prices can be estimated with some precision only over a short time. When predictions extend much beyond a year, forecasts become extremely precarious and will be heavily discounted. The fact that no futures or forward market contract in raw materials extends beyond eighteen months reflects the extreme uncertainties of the forecasts. Unfortunately, the price cycles in many commodities are much longer than a year and a half—perhaps longer than ten years; and they tend to be irregular. (Consider the long price cycles for copper in figure 2, for example.) Private speculators facing the possibility of bankruptcy on the *downside* are not likely to be risk-neutral. They will require a very high risk premium for very risky speculation, i.e., for exactly the longer term speculation required for greater market stabilization. Private speculators must expect very large price increases to compensate for risk if they are to store in anticipation of sales several years hence. As a result, optimal speculation from the private point of view will still permit substantial fluctuations in prices.

Furthermore, one can safely forecast that large shocks to these markets *will* occur: wars (Korea, Mideast, Vietnam, etc.), unusual inflation and recession, associations like OPEC, etc. What cannot be forecast well in advance is the *timing* and *severity* of the shocks. Therefore, private speculators with their risk aversion and fear of downside bankruptcy will be unable in general to dampen price fluctuations from these sources to any appreciable degree. Indeed, speculators may temporarily aggravate the impact of the unexpected shock, as evidence on speculative price run-ups in 1973-74 suggests.

Since unaided private speculation has not dealt and cannot be expected to deal effectively with longer-term price instability, several official sources have proposed producer-consumer commodity agreements to solve the problem.[9] The main tool of such agreements in minerals would be the "buffer stock." In essence, a buffer stock would act as a longer-run supplement to the private market forces of demand and supply. It would buy in periods of glut and sell when private market supplies are unable to prevent large price increases. In principle, a buffer stock need not alter longer-run price trends. Rather, its goal should be to reduce instability around longer-run equilibrium price trends.

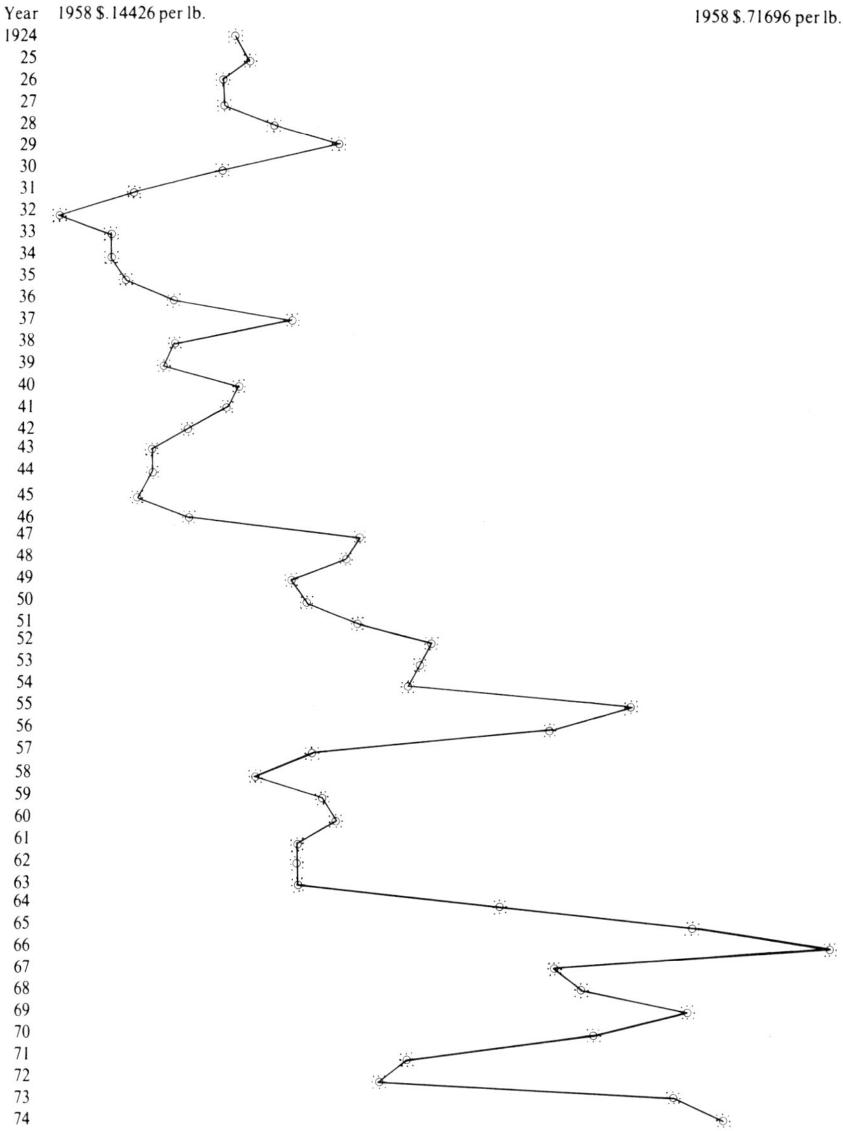

Sources: American Bureau of Metals Statistics, *Yearbook on the London Metals Exchange*, and the *Economic Report of the President*, 1975.

FIG. 2. ANNUAL AVERAGE DOLLAR PRICE OF COPPER (per lb.) on the London Metal Exchange Divided by the U.S. GNP Deflator (1924-1974).

Because they would be publicly financed, with the credit of governments their ultimate guarantee, buffer stocks need not fear bankruptcy nor need they be averse to risk. Thus they could take the longer view and commit more resources to inventories than could the unaided private sector.[10]

Unfortunately, an effective buffer stock has never been tried in primary commodities. It is true that the International Tin Agreement has relied on buffer stocks to a considerable extent, but their size has been so small as to preclude much stabilizing effect.[11] While the idea of buffer stocks may sound attractive, we have little to go on in judging their practical feasibility. How large a stock would be required? How should it be operated? How should it fix the target price around which market prices will be stabilized? Would its benefits outweigh its costs? Some tentative answers to these questions emerge from a study on the desirability of copper buffer stocks.[12]

Copper is one of the more likely candidates for a producer-consumer commodity agreement. It vies with aluminum as the second most important metal in the world (by total value of production). Copper is also especially volatile in price (see figure 2). Macroeconomic instability in the industrial countries is the prime cause of copper price volatility. Copper is used mainly in the manufacture of electrical machinery and equipment—that is, investment goods and consumer durables. Hence the demand for the metal rises and falls with the business cycle, but with considerably greater amplitude than the economy as a whole. Supply is fairly elastic with respect to price within the "normal" range of output, but tends to increasing inelasticity as the extremes of capacity utilization are approached. Thus at least three times in the last twenty years (1954-55, 1964-65, 1973-74) capacity was strained during economic boom and prices skyrocketed; and three times in the ensuing economic recessions prices plummeted below costs.

Supply disturbances have also occurred from time to time. The year 1973, for example, saw civil disturbances in both Chile and Zambia, large suppliers of copper. But as a rule supply shocks have been much less important to copper than to the principal agricultural products, for which weather is crucial.

For the LDCs, copper exports are outdistanced only by export of petroleum. Three countries—Chile, Zambia, and Zaire—depend on copper for well over two-thirds of their foreign exchange earnings (see table 1), and consequently have suffered great and chronic instability in their balance of payments. Almost half of world exports of copper, however, are accounted for by the developed countries, mainly Canada and Australia.

The chief problem with copper for both users and producers is its price instability. Undoubtedly the best way to deal with the problem would be to eliminate its principal cause, the business cycle in the industrial countries. In lieu of this unlikely event, buffer stocks become the main instrument

TABLE 1
SHARES OF LDC EXPORTS OF SIX MINERALS, 1970-1972

Per Capita Income of Major Commodity Exporters		Country Share of World Exports 1970-1972						Commodity Share of Country Exports 1970-1972					
		Bauxite	Copper	Iron Ore	Lead	Tin	Zinc	Bauxite	Copper	Iron Ore	Lead	Tin	Zinc
$0 - 250													
Bolivia	$208[A]				1.48	13.69	1.81				3.74	52.46	7.18
Haiti	80[A]	2.41						15.58					
Liberia	(250)[B]			6.23						72.69			
Mauritania	(180)[B]			2.77						77.16			
Morocco	223				2.69						2.46		
Nigeria	(130)[B]					4.86						2.08	
Sierra Leone	158[C]	2.48						6.51					
Zaire	96.7		9.99			2.64	3.27		68.34			3.00	3.85
India	(110)[B]			5.80						7.13			
Indonesia	106	2.23				8.47		0.49				5.04	
Philippines	242		4.16						16.23				
Thailand	183					10.34						8.84	
Sub-total		7.12	14.15	14.80	4.17	40.0	5.08						
$250 - 500													
Brazil	$395[A]			8.53						7.04			
Dominican Republic	347[A]	5.51						5.67					
Guyana	320[A]	6.91						13.33					
Peru	304[A]		4.63	2.43	6.48		7.08		21.72	6.70	3.34		5.70
Angola	(390)[B]			1.29						7.59			
Zambia	335[C]		17.02		1.42		1.68		94.10		.86		1.60
Malaysia	362	2.16				42.59		0.34				17.87	
Sub-total		14.58	21.65	12.25	7.90	42.59	8.76						
$500 - 1000													
Chile	$564[A]		16.26	2.28					71.60	5.91			
Jamaica	651	32.17						25.47					
Mexico	667[A]				4.31		6.43				1.36		3.17
Venezuels	979			5.27						4.21			
Surinam	(810)[B]	16.55						30.26					
Namibia	723[D]				2.67						25.93		
Sub-total		48.72	16.26	7.55	6.98		6.43						
Total		70.42	52.06	34.60	19.05	82.59	20.27						

Per Capita Income figures are derived from the following sources:
A) 1970-1971 Average; 1973 Statistical Yearbook, United Nations, New York, 1974, p. 590.
B) 1972 GNP per capita; World Bank Atlas: Population, Per Capita and Growth Rates, Washington, D.C., 1974, pp. 12, 14, 18.
C) 1970 only; 1973 Statistical Yearbook, p. 590. D) Per capita income for South Africa, including Namibia; 1973 Statistical Yearbook, p. 590.

Figures pertaining to exports are derived from: Commodity Trade and Price Trends (1974 Edition), Document of the International Bank for Reconstruction and Development, International Development Association, Report No. EC-166/74, pp. 20-25.

which might dampen price volatility without raising prices over the long run. But could a copper buffer stock function effectively? In an attempt to answer this question, we ran simulations of the Charles River Associates-Wharton EFA econometric model of the world copper market, probably the best model of this metal. Our procedure was to introduce a hypothetical buffer stock into the copper market during the historical period 1955-1973. The simulations then determined the buffer stock's impact on prices, consumption, producer revenues, etc., and its cost of operation.

Clearly, simulations of econometric models of the past give imperfect guidance for the future.[13] Market structures will undoubtedly change and the patterns of future economic fluctuations and supply disturbances will not duplicate the past. Still, simulations do permit order of magnitude conclusions, and this is their only goal in the present context.

Before we turn to the simulation results, some discussion of the principles of buffer stock operation is in order. A buffer stock can be described by its rules of buying and selling and the financial resources which are put at its disposal. These, in turn, are determined by the objectives which the buffer stock is designed to achieve. For the present analysis the hypothetical copper buffer stock is designed to stabilize prices within certain bandwidths around *long-run trend prices*. The upper bound on desired prices is called the "ceiling" and the lower bound, the "floor." The long-run trend price is called the "target" price in this paper. The buffer stock sells out of its stock to keep the market price from penetrating the ceiling and buys for inventories when the market price would otherwise go through the floor.

The *bandwidth* of permissible price fluctuations is very important in the operation of a buffer stock. A narrower band will bring greater price stability but will require more buffer stock intervention to defend the floor and ceiling. Very narrow bands also guarantee that the buffer stock will lose money, because the main source of net revenue from the operation is the difference between average buying and selling prices, which will be smaller the narrower the permissible bands of fluctuations. In general, the band should be wide enough to cover interest, storage, and transactions costs. In the simulations we used three alternative bandwidths: ± 5%, 7.5%, and 10% centered on target prices.

The choice of each year's target price is critical. If the target is consistently set above long-term equilibrium values, the buffer stock will be a net purchaser of copper, will suffer large financial losses, and will distort resource allocation. On the other hand, target prices far below long-run trend values mean that the buffer stock will rarely purchase copper to defend the floor, and hence will have insufficient stocks to defend the ceiling. The buffer stock will make a profit, but will have minor impact in reducing price fluctuations.

How should the target price be set? Preferably, at its "long-run trend" value according to the objectives of the buffer stock; but in practice this is an ambiguous concept and one difficult to estimate. Five year lagged moving averages, adjusted annually, are one estimate of trend price which commends itself as a rule of thumb, mainly because of its simplicity and ease of application.[14] We use it in the simulations. It allows some accommodation to recent market forces, but greatly dilutes current events as indicators of longer-term trends. Steady upward or downward pressure would show up as steady upward or downward movements in the lagged moving average.

Obviously, there are many other methods of estimating trend prices, and even the five-year length of the moving average is somewhat arbitrary. As will be seen below, however, this simple rule of thumb worked quite well in the simulations, so that there was no need to pursue more complicated approaches.

Unfortunately, the five-year moving average rule could not be used in setting the initial (1955) target price for simulation. The five years prior to 1955 included the commodity boom provoked by the Korean War scare. Average prices over the period 1950-1954 were far above long-run trend. We chose instead an initial target of 1967 \$.45 per lb. of copper wirebar—a moderate support price fairly close to the full cost of production at that time. The weight given to market prices in calculating the target increased each year from 1956 to 1960, and by 1961 the five-year lagged moving average rule was in full force.

Finally, the question must be asked: which market price should be the target of the buffer stock operation? During the period simulated (1955-1973), the London Metals Exchange (LME) price of copper wirebar was the basis for transactions in all the world except the United States.[15] Thus it was used as the basis for calculating the target. The pound price was converted into dollars at 1967 exchange rates and then deflated by the U.S. wholesale price index. This procedure in effect *indexes* the target price. Real price, rather than nominal price, is the target.

To recapitulate, the buffer stock is simulated over the period 1955-1973. The operation buys and sells to maintain prices within three alternative bands ±5%, 7.5%, and 10% around target price, which in turn is calculated as the five-year moving average, lagged one year, of the real LME dollar price of copper. In order to determine the financial requirements of each rule, the buffer stock is assumed to have unlimited capital resources.

A summary of the simulation results is presented in table 2 and figure 3. They show that relatively simple buffer stock rules could have brought dramatic reductions in price fluctuations during the simulation period without great social cost. True, the ±5% band is much too narrow, and as a result loses \$850 million (in 1967 prices). Discounted real buffer stock losses in the 10% simulation, however, were quite moderate, averaging \$13 million per year over the 1955-1973 period. To give some idea of relative size, a .3%

TABLE 2

Simulations of the Impact of Hypothetical Buffer Stock to Maintain Price Within ±5, 7.5, 10% Around 5-Year Lagged Moving Average, 1955-1973

Initial Price = 1967 $.45/lb.

Variable/Simulation	5%	7.5%	10%
Real LME Copper Price in $[1]			
Largest Percentage Annual Increase	9.3	12.8	41.8
Largest Percentage Annual Decrease	-7.9	-12.2	-13.1
Average Annual Percentage Increase	3.0	4.7	8.5
Average Annual Percentage Decrease	-2.7	-3.5	4.6
Discounted Real Producer Revenue (billion 1967 $)[2]	66.40	65.22	65.44
Percent Revenue differs from no buffer stock activity simulation	-3.8	-5.5	-5.1
Discounted Real Buffer[3] Profit (million 1967 $)	-847.9	-508.5	-208.5
Maximum Stock Reached (th. s. t.)	5450.6	4759.8	4020.7
Maximum Investment in Stock (1967 $ million)	4552.2	3703.8	2892.0
Average Investment (1967 $)	2531.6	1934.5	1350.5
Terminal Stock (th. s. t.)	1169.1	154.6	0

Notes:

1. The LME price was converted to dollars and then deflated by the BLS Wholesale Price Index.
2. 2% real discount rate, 1% ad valorem transactions costs and .65% ad valorem annual storage costs were assumed.
3. (Sales minus purchases minus storage and transactions costs), all in 1967 $ and discounted back to 1955, the beginning year of the buffer stock.

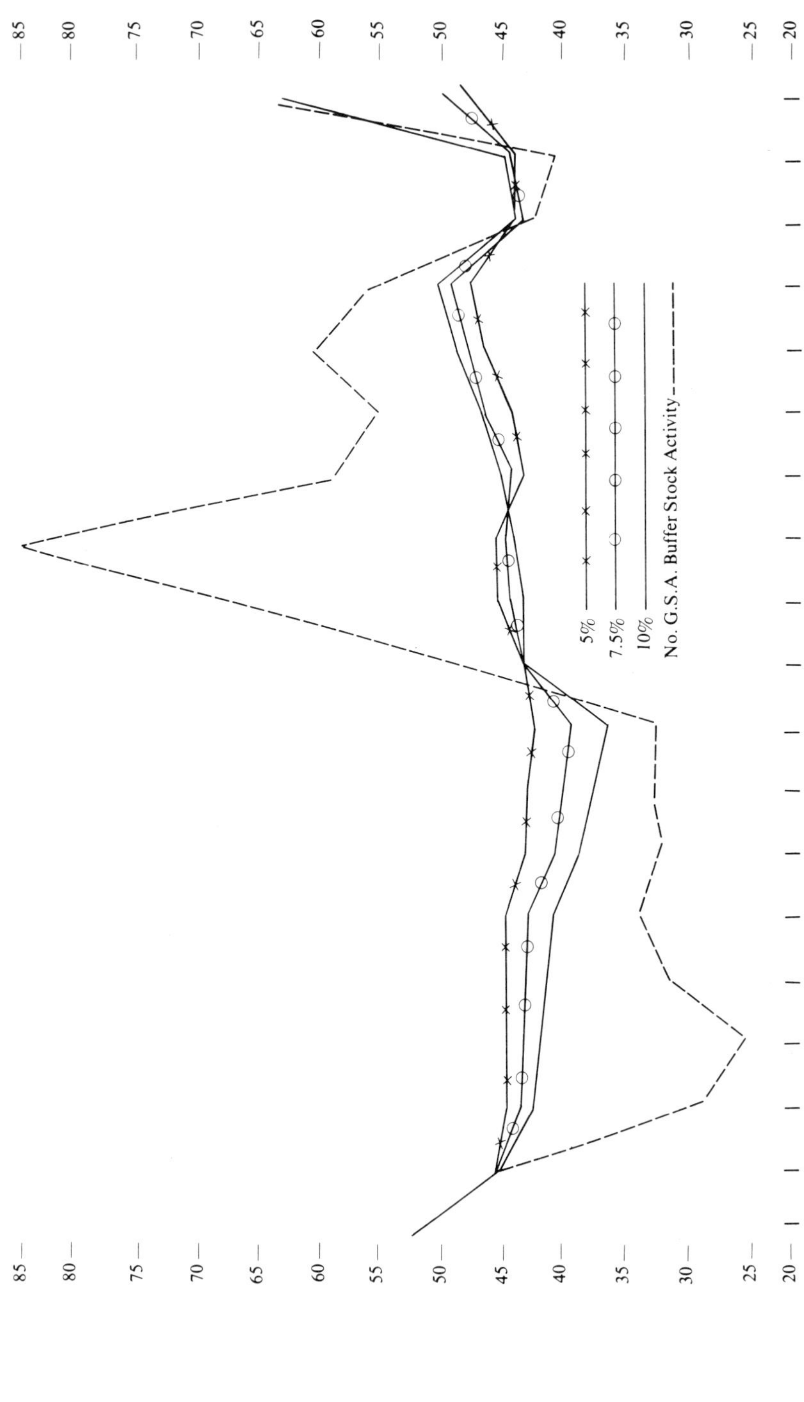

FIG. 3. SIMULATED LME PRICE 1967 cents per lb. Buffer stock rule to maintain price within ±5%, ±7.5%, and ±10% bands of lagged moving average.

tax on the discounted value of world copper sales would have sufficed to pay for losses under the 10% rule. Work not yet completed suggests that a ±15% rule would actually have made a profit, but at the cost of greater price instability.

The simulations give considerable support to those who argue that a long-term copper agreement to stabilize prices within some band (something like ±10% seems most reasonable) around price trends would bring substantial improvement in the operation of the copper market at very little cost. It would have to be understood from the beginning that price *stabilization*, not artificial increases in long-run copper prices, would be the goal of the agreement. Production and export controls would not be permitted in the agreement. The initial target price should be set as closely as possible to long-run equilibrium prices.[16] Then some mechanical rule, such as the "crawling peg" (five year moving average) used in the simulation, should be used to adjust target prices annually.

The main, and probably decisive, factors militating against such an agreement are the size of the financial commitment and the patience that would be required of the parties to the pact. In the simulations, a total investment on the order of $3 billion (in 1967 prices) was tied up in copper stocks for several years running. At its maximum, the buffer stock held in storage sufficient copper to satisfy all demands (except from communist countries) for the metal for at least eight months. This amount is much larger than the figures mentioned by the proponents of a copper agreement, and it would be extremely difficult to negotiate an agreement of such magnitude.

In the simulations, the first sale from stock took place only in 1965, in the *eleventh year* of the agreement. Until that time, all operations had been in support of the copper price floor. Surely by that time the consumer member nations would have begun to suspect that the agreement was stacked in favor of copper producers. Probably the consumer nations would have forced large reductions in the target price, which would have reduced the effectiveness of the agreement over the long run,[17] or perhaps the agreement would have collapsed. Other work which has been done with tin, lead, and zinc led to qualitatively similar conclusions to those reported for the copper in this paper.[18]

In a sense, the conclusions of the analysis are both optimistic and pessimistic. There does appear to be real foundation to the notion that both consumers and producers—both industrial and less developed countries—could benefit from the right type of commodity agreement, but the "right" type requires all sides to be far more forthcoming in financial resources than they are likely to be. "Façade" agreements, such as those we have had in tin and coffee, are thus likely to be the result. The ineffectiveness of façade agreements would soon be exposed by market forces, probably amidst bitter recriminations from all sides.

NOTES

This paper was written while the author was a senior international economist at the U. S. Treasury. I would like to thank Thomas D. Willett for helpful encouragement and George R. Schink of Wharton EFA for running the simulations of the copper buffer stock.

1. See, for example, *World Economic Interdependence and Trade in Commodities,* presented to Parliament by the Prime Minister, May 1975, especially pp. 1-15; UNCTAD, *An Integrated Programme for Commodities*, TD/B/C.1/166, 9 December 1974.

2. See, for example, UNCTAD, "The Indexation of Prices," TD/B/503, 6 August 1974; Sixth U. N. General Assembly "Declaration of the Establishment of a New International Economic Order."

3. The first UNCTAD meeting in 1964 was the source of much of the content of the "New Order."

4. After OPEC refused to talk oil alone at the first petroleum producer-consumer conference in the spring of 1975, the consumer nations finally relented in their insistence on separating oil from other raw materials.

5. See C. Fred Bergsten, "The Threat from the Third World," *Foreign Policy* **11**, pp. 102-124.

6. This has been the case in the Coffee Agreement, for example, since its inception in 1962.

7. Chile is perhaps the most extreme case. It depends upon copper for two-thirds of its foreign exchange earnings.

8. This scenario assumes that there are no externalities from price fluctuations and that all prices accurately reflect social benefits and costs. Both assumptions have been attacked, but their accuracy is not crucial for the present discussion. I argue that even without externalities and market distortions, private speculation will be suboptimal.

9. Commodity agreements are an important part of the European Economic Community, the UNCTAD, and the English proposals. France has long favored commodity agreements, while the U. S. has generally opposed them.

10. One *could* design re-insurance or loan availability programs which could greatly reduce downside risk to private speculators. These programs, "subsidies" to speculation, would almost certainly be politically unacceptable.

11. See Gordon W. Smith and George Schink, "The International Tin Agreement: A Reassessment," U. S. Treasury OASIA Discussion Paper, July 1975.

12. See Gordon W. Smith, "Internationally Held Buffer Stocks," U. S. Treasury-OASIA Research, April 29, 1975 (mimeograph).

13. One wag has defined econometrics as: "a field of economics which specializes in predicting the past with ever increasing accuracy."

14. The target price for the current year is estimated as the average of the previous five years. Next year's trend price is calculated by adding this year's price and dropping that of six years ago, and so forth.

15. Most transactions in the U. S. take place at the producer's "list" price, which is not market clearing.

16. \$.70/lb. of copper wirebar is often suggested.

17. This would have been equivalent to widening the band of permissible price fluctuation.

18. See Smith, "Internationally Held Buffer Stocks."